Cybersecurity Unveiled

The Art of Cyber Defense:
A Comprehensive Guide to Protecting Your Data

Benjamin Chang

© Copyright 2023 - All rights reserved.

The content contained within this book may not be reproduced, duplicated or transmitted without direct written permission from the author or the publisher.

Under no circumstances will any blame or legal responsibility be held against the publisher, or author, for any damages, reparation, or monetary loss due to the information contained within this book, either directly or indirectly.

Legal Notice:

This book is copyright protected. It is only for personal use. You cannot amend, distribute, sell, use, quote or paraphrase any part, or the content within this book, without the consent of the author or publisher.

Disclaimer Notice:

Please note the information contained within this document is for educational and entertainment purposes only. All effort has been executed to present accurate, up to date, reliable, complete information. No warranties of any kind are declared or implied. Readers acknowledge that the author is not engaging in the rendering of legal, financial, medical or professional advice. The content within this book has been derived from various sources. Please consult a licensed professional before attempting any techniques outlined in this book.

By reading this document, the reader agrees that under no circumstances is the author responsible for any losses, direct or indirect, that are incurred as a result of the use of information contained within this document, including, but not limited to, errors, omissions, or inaccuracies.

Table of Contents

INTRODUCTION 6

CHAPTER I: Understanding Cyber Threats 8

    Types of cyber threats: malware, phishing, ransomware, etc. 8

    Real-world examples of major cyber attacks 10

    The evolving landscape of cyber threats 13

CHAPTER II: Foundations of Cyber Defense 16

    Explaining the CIA Triad: Confidentiality, Integrity, Availability 16

    Role of encryption in data protection 18

    Basics of access controls and authentication 21

CHAPTER III: Securing Your Devices 24

    Best practices for securing computers, smartphones, and tablets 24

    Importance of regular software updates 27

    Implementing strong passwords and two-factor authentication 29

CHAPTER IV: Safe Internet Practices 33

    Recognizing phishing emails and websites 33

    Using secure and private browsing 36

    Safe social media usage and privacy settings 38

CHAPTER V: Data Protection Measures 43

    Importance of data backup and recovery strategies 43

    Exploring cloud storage security 46

    Data retention policies and data disposal practices 49

CHAPTER VI: Network Security 53

    Understanding firewalls and intrusion detection/prevention systems 53

    Wireless network security tips 56

    Virtual Private Networks (VPNs) for secure connections 60

CHAPTER VII: Application Security 64

    Securing web applications and APIs 64

    The role of secure coding practices 67

    Common vulnerabilities and how to mitigate them 71

CHAPTER VIII: Security for Small Businesses 75

    Cybersecurity considerations for small business owners 75

    Building a cybersecurity policy and incident response plan 78

    Protecting customer data and maintaining trust 81

CHAPTER IX: Emerging Technologies and Threats 86

    Exploring AI-driven cybersecurity solutions 86

    Risks and benefits of IoT devices 89

Potential impact of quantum computing on cybersecurity 92

CHAPTER X: Government Regulations and Compliance . 96

Overview of cybersecurity regulations (e.g., GDPR, HIPAA) 96

Navigating compliance requirements 100

Consequences of non-compliance 103

CHAPTER XI: Building a Cybersecurity Mindset 108

Fostering a culture of cybersecurity awareness 108

Continuous learning and staying updated on threats . 111

Encouraging responsible online behavior 115

CHAPTER XII: The Future of Cybersecurity 120

Predictions for the future of cybersecurity 120

Ethical considerations in cybersecurity research and practices 123

Encouraging innovation while prioritizing security 126

CONCLUSION 131

Recap of key takeaways from the book 131

Encouragement for readers to implement cybersecurity practices 133

Final thoughts on the importance of cyber defense ... 136

INTRODUCTION

In the age of digital connectivity, where every facet of our lives is intertwined with technology, the significance of cybersecurity cannot be overstated. Welcome to "Cybersecurity Unveiled: The Art of Cyber Defense - A Comprehensive Guide to Protecting Your Data." Knowing how to protect your information has become a crucial life skill in our quickly changing digital environment where data breaches and cyber threats loom larger than ever.

Think about a society where your private information, financial information, and conversations are no longer secure. Unfortunately, such a world is more nearby than we might realize. Our digital lives are in danger as cybercriminals aggressively search for weaknesses to attack using innovative methods and tools. There has never been a more pressing necessity to strengthen our defenses and keep one step ahead.

This in-depth book aims to arm you with the information and resources required to traverse the intricate world of cybersecurity successfully. This book is your travel companion as you transition to cyber resilience, whether you're an individual looking to safeguard your personal data, a business owner looking to protect customer information, or just curious about the systems that support our digital security.

We'll delve into the intricacies of cyber threats throughout these pages, from the well-known phishing emails to the complex ransomware attacks that grab headlines. We'll go through the fundamentals of cybersecurity and walk you through the fundamentals of network protection, safe internet usage, and device security, among other things. By the time you reach the conclusion, you'll have a firm understanding of the risks we face and the tactics to combat them.

Cybersecurity demands constant monitoring, flexibility, and a mindset focused on safety; it is not a one-time effort. As you start this learning journey, remember that every little action you do to protect your online presence adds to the overall effort to make the internet a safer place for everyone.

So, let's start exploring the art of cybersecurity. Together, we'll learn the strategies, resources, and guidelines to let you master the digital world and take charge of your life online.

CHAPTER I

Understanding Cyber Threats

Types of cyber threats: malware, phishing, ransomware, etc.

In today's interconnected world, the digital landscape is a gateway to endless possibilities and a realm of lurking threats. As our reliance on technology deepens, so does the sophistication of cyber threats that seek to exploit vulnerabilities and compromise our sensitive information. This section delves into some of the most prominent cyber threats, shedding light on their mechanisms, impacts, and measures to defend against them.

Malware, also known as malicious software, is a broad term encompassing a range of software programs designed with harmful intent. From viruses and worms to Trojans and spyware, malware takes various forms, each with a unique modus operandi. Viruses attach themselves to legitimate files, spreading and infecting others upon execution. Worms, conversely, are standalone programs that replicate and spread independently. Trojans masquerade as benign software, enticing users to install them, only to unleash their malicious payload once activated. Spyware silently monitors and gathers information about users' activities, while adware bombards users with unwanted advertisements. Regardless of the type, malware poses a significant threat, compromising data integrity, stealing sensitive information, and granting unauthorized access to cybercriminals.

Phishing is a cyber threat that preys on human psychology rather than exploiting technical vulnerabilities. It involves sending deceptive emails, messages, or websites masquerading as legitimate entities to trick recipients into divulging sensitive information, like the credit card details, passwords, or personal identification. These phishing attempts often appear to be from trustworthy sources, like financial institutions or well-known companies, and use urgency or fear tactics to prompt swift action. The rise of sophisticated spear phishing attacks further targets specific individuals or organizations, using tailored messages to increase the likelihood of success. Phishing exploits our inherent trust in digital communication, emphasizing the need for constant vigilance and education to identify and thwart such attempts.

Ransomware has emerged as one of the most financially lucrative and disruptive cyber threats. This malicious software encrypts a victim's data, rendering it inaccessible until a ransom is paid to the attackers, often in cryptocurrency. Ransomware attacks can have devastating implications for individuals and organizations alike. In 2017, the WannaCry ransomware attack affected hundreds of thousands of computers worldwide, exploiting a vulnerability in outdated software. The attack paralyzed hospitals, businesses, and government institutions, illustrating the far-reaching impact of ransomware. The evolution of ransomware tactics includes double extortion, where attackers encrypt the victim's data and threaten to divulge it unless the ransom is paid. Preventing ransomware requires a multi-pronged approach: regular software updates, robust data backups, and proactive security measures.

Beyond these primary threats, the cyber landscape continues to evolve, introducing new challenges and complexities. Distributed Denial of Service attacks, also referred to as DDoS attacks, flood a target system with overwhelming traffic, rendering it inaccessible to users. Advanced Persistent Threats (APTs) are highly sophisticated, long-term attacks often orchestrated by state-sponsored actors or skilled hacking groups. Insider threats involve individuals with privileged access to an organization's systems or data who misuse that access for personal gain or harm. Internet of Things (IoT) vulnerabilities arise from insecure smart devices that can be exploited to gain unauthorized access to networks or compromise user privacy.

In the face of these diverse and ever-evolving threats, a proactive and multi-layered approach to cybersecurity is imperative. Regular software updates and patches help mitigate vulnerabilities that attackers exploit. Strong and unique passwords, combined with two-factor authentication, enhance access control. Employee education and awareness campaigns empower individuals to recognize and report suspicious activities. Moreover, adopting a security-first mindset and staying informed about emerging threats are crucial components of a robust cyber defense strategy.

In conclusion, as our lives become increasingly intertwined with technology, the threat landscape expands and diversifies. Malware, phishing, ransomware, and many other cyber threats challenge our digital security and privacy. While technology empowers us, it also demands that we remain vigilant, informed, and proactive in safeguarding our digital lives. By understanding these threats, their mechanisms, and the steps to counter them, we can navigate the digital realm with confidence and resilience. Cybersecurity is not merely an option; it's a necessity in our modern world.

Real-world examples of major cyber attacks

In the ever-expanding digital landscape, where our lives are intricately woven into the fabric of technology, cyber attacks have emerged as a formidable threat. Cyber attacks, ranging from the simple to the highly sophisticated, can disrupt economies, compromise personal data, and challenge the very foundations of our interconnected world. This section delves into real-world examples of major cyber attacks that have left an unforgettable mark on the global stage, highlighting their methods, impacts, and the lessons they impart.

The Stuxnet worm, discovered in 2010, marked a significant turning point in cyber warfare. Widely attributed to a joint effort by U.S. and Israeli intelligence agencies, Stuxnet was designed with a singular purpose: to sabotage Iran's nuclear program by targeting its uranium enrichment centrifuges. This worm exploited multiple zero-day vulnerabilities to propagate within the target's systems, ultimately causing severe damage to many centrifuges. Stuxnet demonstrated the potential of cyber attacks to cause physical destruction and highlighted the need for heightened security measures for critical infrastructure.

In 2014, the Sony Pictures hack exposed a new dimension of cyber attacks—cyber espionage with political motivations. Attributed to North Korea in response to the film "The Interview," which portrayed the country's leader in a satirical light, the attack compromised vast amounts of internal data. This included unreleased films, executive emails, and personal information of employees. The incident underscored the reach of cyber attacks beyond financial gains, serving as a reminder that cyber warfare can have far-reaching diplomatic and cultural ramifications.

The 2017 Equifax data breach highlighted the immense impact of compromising personal data. The breach reveal sensitive information, including social security numbers, birthdates, and addresses, of nearly 147 million individuals. The fallout from the breach was profound, leading to identity theft, financial losses, and a significant erosion of public trust. Equifax's mishandling of the incident further exemplified the importance of timely and transparent communication in the aftermath of a cyber attack.

NotPetya, a ransomware attack that struck in 2017, demonstrated the potential for cyber attacks to cascade into widespread disruption. Initially disguised as ransomware, NotPetya was later revealed to be a state-sponsored attack attributed to Russia. It targeted Ukraine, but its propagation mechanism quickly spread the malware globally. Numerous organizations, including major corporations, experienced downtime and financial losses. NotPetya highlighted the interconnectedness of our digital ecosystem and the potential for collateral damage in cyber conflicts.

The SolarWinds supply chain attack, discovered in 2020, highlighted the insidious nature of targeting trusted software vendors. Attackers compromised SolarWinds' software updates, injecting malicious code that was subsequently distributed to thousands of customers, including U.S. government agencies and major tech companies. This highly sophisticated attack showcased the attackers' patience and meticulous planning, and the scale of its impact underscored the need for comprehensive security assessments throughout the supply chain.

These examples offer a glimpse into the diverse landscape of cyber attacks, each with its distinct motives, methods, and implications. They collectively emphasize the urgency of strengthening cyber defenses and fostering a culture of cybersecurity awareness. The lessons drawn from these incidents are clear: cyber attacks transcend borders, industries, and motivations. No entity, whether governmental, corporate, or individual, is immune to their impact.

As we progress, the imperative to bolster our cybersecurity measures becomes more pressing than ever. Collaborative efforts between governments, private sectors, and individuals are essential to fortify our digital infrastructure. Cyber attacks are not mere anomalies; they are the new reality of our interconnected world. By understanding these real-world examples, we gain insights into the evolving tactics of cyber adversaries and pave the way for a safer, more resilient digital future.

The evolving landscape of cyber threats

In the intricate realm between innovation and vulnerability, the digital era has ushered in remarkable advancements alongside unprecedented risks. The cyber threats landscape is constantly evolving, shaped by the ingenuity of cybercriminals, the expanding digital footprint, and the relentless pursuit of technological progress. This section delves into cyber threats' dynamic and multifaceted nature, tracing their evolution, exploring emerging challenges, and highlighting the imperative for adaptive cybersecurity strategies.

The origins of cyber threats can be traced back to the internet's nascent days when hackers sought bragging rights through feats like defacing websites. As technology matured, so did cybercriminals' methods. The transition from isolated attacks to organized cybercrime syndicates marked a pivotal shift, leading to the rise of malware, phishing, and identity theft. With the advent of cryptocurrencies, a new avenue emerged for ransomware attacks that could be executed anonymously. Cyber warfare also gained traction, as nation-states recognized the potential to destroy adversaries' critical infrastructure without deploying conventional military forces.

The digital landscape is expanding, and with it, the attack surface for cybercriminals. The Internet of Things (IoT) devices proliferation, smart cities, and interconnected industrial systems introduces novel vulnerabilities. IoT devices, ranging from smart thermostats to medical devices, often lack robust security measures, making them susceptible to hijacking for botnets and DDoS attacks. As critical infrastructure becomes increasingly connected, the potential for disruptive attacks on power grids, transportation systems, and water supplies amplifies. This expansion of attack vectors necessitates a comprehensive approach to cybersecurity that goes beyond traditional perimeter defenses.

The emergence of state-sponsored cyber attacks has blurred the lines between traditional warfare and digital conflict. Nation-states invest heavily in cyber capabilities, utilizing them for espionage, sabotage, and geopolitical manipulation. The Stuxnet worm, thought to be a joint U.S.-Israeli creation, demonstrated the potential for cyber attacks to damage infrastructure physically. Nation-states also use disinformation campaigns, leveraging social media platforms to spread propaganda and sow discord. The cyber arms race has redefined the concept of conflict, prompting discussions about the rules of engagement in this intangible battleground.

Advanced Persistent Threats (APTs) exemplify the intricate strategies deployed by cyber adversaries. APTs are sustained and targeted attacks, often originating from state-sponsored actors or organized crime groups. These attacks are characterized by their stealthy nature, with intruders maintaining a low profile over extended periods to gather sensitive information. APTs commonly leverage zero-day vulnerabilities—previously unknown software vulnerabilities—for maximum impact. The trade in zero-day exploits has fueled a shadowy economy, raising ethical questions about the responsible disclosure of vulnerabilities versus their potential weaponization.

The evolution of cyber threats is inextricably linked to technological innovation. As machine learning and artificial intelligence advance, so do their applications in cyber attacks. AI-powered malware can adapt and evade traditional defenses, while ML algorithms analyze massive datasets to uncover patterns for highly effective phishing campaigns. Additionally, quantum computing's promise of exponential processing power could render existing encryption methods obsolete, requiring a paradigm shift in cryptography. Integrating 5G networks further accelerates the proliferation of IoT devices and introduces new security challenges.

The urgency to develop proactive and adaptive cybersecurity strategies cannot be overstated in navigating this evolving landscape. Traditional defensive measures are no longer enough in a world where attacks can come from anywhere on the globe. Cybersecurity must be integrated into every layer of technology and business operations. Collaboration among governments, private industries, and academia is essential for knowledge sharing and response coordination. Furthermore, cultivating a culture of cybersecurity awareness among individuals and organizations is paramount to reducing the human element of cyber vulnerability.

In conclusion, the evolving landscape of cyber threats reflects the relentless march of progress intertwined with human ingenuity. The digital realm is a playground for innovation but also a battlefield where the battle lines are constantly shifting. As our reliance on technology deepens, the imperative to understand, adapt to, and defend against cyber threats becomes non-negotiable. The future will undoubtedly bring novel challenges and opportunities, demanding that we remain vigilant, resilient, and committed to safeguarding the digital domain that shapes every facet of modern life.

CHAPTER II

Foundations of Cyber Defense

Explaining the CIA Triad: Confidentiality, Integrity, Availability

In the sprawling landscape of cyberspace, where information flows seamlessly and the boundaries between the physical and digital worlds blur, the need for comprehensive cybersecurity principles has become more pressing than ever. Enter the CIA Triad—a foundational framework that forms the bedrock of modern cybersecurity practices. The CIA Triad, which consists of Confidentiality, Integrity, and Availability, provides a structured way of protecting data, systems, and networks from the various threats that permeate the digital landscape. This section delves into the nuances of each component, illustrating their significance and collective role in fortifying our digital defenses.

Confidentiality lies at the heart of data protection, ensuring that sensitive information stays accessible only to authorized individuals. Maintaining confidentiality is paramount in a world where personal, financial, and intellectual data are the lifeblood of business and society. Encryption, one of the cornerstones of confidentiality, transforms data into an unreadable format unless accessed with the appropriate decryption key. Secure access controls and authentication mechanisms bolster confidentiality, preventing unauthorized entry to digital spaces. Confidentiality aligns with the principle of limiting "need-to-know" access, ensuring that individuals access only the data required to fulfill their roles.

Integrity focuses on the reliability and accuracy of data. It ensures that information remains unaltered and authentic, reflecting its actual state. Data integrity is crucial for business operations, the veracity of digital transactions, and the preservation of historical records. Hash functions and digital signatures are cryptographic techniques that validate data integrity. Hashing converts data into a fixed-size string of characters, while digital signatures use asymmetric encryption to authenticate the sender's identity and verify data integrity. By assuring data integrity, organizations can rely on the accuracy of the information they store and transmit, fostering trust among stakeholders.

Availability underscores the necessity of making resources and data accessible when needed. Ensuring continuous availability is paramount in a digital ecosystem where downtime can translate to financial losses, reputation damage, and even public safety risks. Redundancy and fault-tolerant systems mitigate the impact of hardware failures, while disaster recovery and business continuity plans prepare organizations for catastrophic events. DDoS (Distributed Denial of Service) attacks, which inundate systems with overwhelming traffic, pose a significant threat to availability. Mitigation techniques, such as traffic filtering and load balancing, counteract these attacks, ensuring uninterrupted services.

The interplay of these three principles constitutes the foundation of the CIA Triad, creating a holistic approach to cybersecurity. However, these principles are not standalone entities; they intersect and overlap, reinforcing one another to create a robust defense posture. Confidentiality may rely on encryption to maintain privacy, which requires data integrity to prevent tampering with encrypted content. Data availability is intertwined with confidentiality and integrity, as users need access to accurate and unaltered information.

While the CIA Triad provides a robust framework, its application is challenging. Balancing security with usability is delicate, as stringent security measures can sometimes hinder user experience. Additionally, rapid technological advancements introduce novel vulnerabilities that may not align neatly with the traditional CIA framework. For instance, the appearance of cloud computing has necessitated reevaluations of data ownership and control.

In conclusion, the CIA Triad is more than a theoretical construct; it is a fundamental approach to safeguarding the digital realm. Confidentiality, Integrity, and Availability collectively create a tapestry of defense against the myriad cyber threats that persistently seek to compromise our data, systems, and networks. Embracing the principles of the CIA Triad requires a comprehensive understanding of the digital landscape, an adaptive mindset, and a commitment to continuous improvement. As the world becomes increasingly interconnected, these principles offer a steadfast guide to navigating the ever-evolving landscape of cybersecurity, ensuring that our digital assets remain secure, trustworthy, and accessible to those who rely on them.

Role of encryption in data protection

In the age of digital connectivity, where the boundaries between the physical and digital landscape are increasingly blurred, the need for robust data protection has never been more pronounced. As sensitive information traverses the vast expanse of the internet, the specter of cyber threats looms large. Amidst this backdrop of vulnerability, encryption stands as a stalwart guardian, a cryptographic shield that safeguards our data from prying eyes and potential breaches. This section explores the multifaceted role of encryption in data protection, delving into its mechanisms, applications, and the broader consequences for privacy and security.

Encryption is the art of transforming readable data into an unreadable format, known as ciphertext, using complex mathematical algorithms. This transformation uses an encryption key, a unique sequence of characters that serves as a digital lock. Encryption keys hold the power to both encrypt and decrypt data, ensuring that only those possessing the correct key can access the original information. The strength of encryption lies in its mathematical complexity, making it computationally infeasible for unauthorized parties to reverse the process and decipher the ciphertext without the appropriate key.

Confidentiality, the first component of the CIA Triad, is at the heart of encryption's purpose. When encrypted, sensitive information remains shielded from prying eyes, even if intercepted during transmission or compromised in storage. As a result, encryption is the cornerstone of secure communication channels, preventing eavesdropping and unauthorized access. From financial transactions and personal messages to corporate communications, encryption acts as a digital envelope, preserving the contents' privacy.

Encryption's reach extends beyond the virtual realm, encompassing data at rest and in transit. Data-at-rest encryption secures information stored on physical devices such as hard drives, ensuring that even if a device is stolen or lost, the data remains indecipherable without the encryption key. Data-in-transit encryption safeguards data as it travels between devices and over networks, thwarting potential interceptors. Secure Sockets Layer (SSL) as well as Transport Layer Security (TLS) protocols, commonly used for online transactions and communication, rely on encryption to create secure connections.

While confidentiality is encryption's primary focus, data integrity is an inherent byproduct. The cryptographic transformation that encryption employs not only keeps data hidden but also ensures that it remains unaltered during transmission or storage. This aspect of encryption protects against unauthorized modifications or tampering of data. In a world where the accuracy of information is paramount, such as financial transactions or medical records, the role of encryption in preserving data integrity is invaluable.

Encryption is a powerful tool, but its implementation is challenging. The proliferation of encrypted data can potentially hinder law enforcement investigations, leading to debates around "going dark." Additionally, the complexity of encryption algorithms requires robust key management practices to prevent loss or unauthorized access to keys. Poorly implemented encryption, such as using weak algorithms or insecure key storage, can lead to a false sense of security.

As technology advances, so does the complexity of cyber threats and the need for robust data protection. Quantum computing, with its potential to break existing encryption methods, raises questions about the long-term efficacy of current encryption standards. In response, researchers are exploring quantum-resistant encryption methods. The tension between security and privacy remains a central theme, as debates about encryption backdoors and lawful intercepts continue. Striking the right balance between enabling legal investigations and preserving individual privacy remains a complex challenge.

In conclusion, encryption is the digital equivalent of a fortress, offering a protective shield for our sensitive information in an age of digital vulnerability. Its role extends beyond mere secrecy, encompassing data integrity and security. Encryption underpins secure communication, bolsters data protection regulations, and empowers individuals to control their digital footprint. As technology evolves and threats diversify, encryption remains an enduring tool in the fight against cybercrime. Its complex algorithms and keys represent a commitment to a safer digital future, where our information is concealed and safeguarded with mathematical certainty.

Basics of access controls and authentication

In the intricate realm of cybersecurity, where digital boundaries intersect with the vast information landscape, access controls and authentication are the bedrock of secure data management. In a world teeming with cyber threats and data breaches, the need to restrict entry to sensitive resources and verify the identity of users has become paramount. This section delves into the fundamental principles of access controls and authentication, unraveling their intricacies, exploring their applications, and highlighting their role in fortifying the digital realm.

Access controls serve as the virtual gates that determine who is allowed entry to a digital domain, be it a network, a system, or a file. These controls are implemented through a combination of technical and organizational measures, each contributing to the overall security posture. The principle of least privilege, a foundational concept, dictates that users should be granted only the permissions necessary to fulfill their roles, minimizing potential damage from compromised accounts. Role-based access control (RBAC) refines this concept by assigning permissions based on job roles or functions. Access controls can be discretionary, allowing users to determine access to their own resources, or mandatory, enforced by system administrators.

Authentication is verifying the identity of users or entities seeking access to a system or resource. It ensures that the entity attempting access is who they claim to be. In the digital realm, authentication relies on the use of credentials, typically a combination of something the user knows (e.g., a password), something they have (e.g., a security token), or something they are (e.g., biometric features like fingerprints or facial recognition). Multi- factor authentication (MFA) strengthens security by requiring multiple verification forms, mitigating the risk of compromised passwords. Biometric authentication, with its unique physiological traits, offers convenience and security.

Various access control models provide structured frameworks for managing permissions and restrictions. The Discretionary Access Control (DAC) model allows users to determine access to their resources, while Mandatory Access Control (MAC) enforces strict access based on predefined security labels. Role-Based Access Control (RBAC) associates permissions with specific roles, simplifying administration. Attribute-Based Access Control (ABAC) considers a range of attributes, such as user roles and environmental conditions, to make access decisions. These models offer organizations flexibility in tailoring access controls to their specific needs and security requirements.

While access controls and authentication are fundamental to cybersecurity, their effective implementation is not without challenges. While widely used, password-based authentication is susceptible to breaches due to weak passwords, password reuse, and phishing attacks. Biometric authentication, although robust, raises privacy concerns related to data storage and potential misuse. Striking a balance between strong security and user experience is another challenge; overly stringent access controls can hinder productivity, while lax controls expose organizations to risk.

As technology evolves, so do the methods of access controls and authentication. Continuous authentication leverages behavioral biometrics, analyzing user behaviors like typing patterns and mouse movements, to create a seamless and ongoing verification process. Zero Trust architecture assumes that no user or device can be fully trusted, requiring strict authentication and authorization for every access attempt. Passwordless authentication, which eliminates the need for traditional passwords, relies on cryptographic keys, biometrics, or other secure mechanisms.

Access controls and authentication extend beyond technical considerations to ethical and legal dimensions. Organizations are responsible for protecting user data, ensuring that authentication and access control mechanisms don't compromise privacy. Regulatory frameworks, for instance, the General Data Protection Regulation, which is also referred to as GDPR, dictate stringent requirements for securing personal data and controlling access to it. The ethical use of biometric data, in particular, requires transparency and informed consent.

In conclusion, access controls and authentication are the digital gatekeepers, regulating entry to the virtual realm and ensuring that only authorized users gain access to sensitive resources. These principles are more than just technical mechanisms; they shape the fabric of cybersecurity, determining the security posture of individuals, organizations, and even entire nations. As the digital landscape evolves and threats diversify, access controls and authentication remain the first line of defense against data breaches, cyber attacks, and unauthorized access. By embracing these foundational concepts, we lay the groundwork for a safer and more secure digital future, where information flows freely only to those with the digital keys of legitimacy.

CHAPTER III

Securing Your Devices

Best practices for securing computers, smartphones, and tablets

The imperative to safeguard these devices from cyber threats has taken center stage in a world characterized by digital interconnectedness, where computers, smartphones, and tablets are our windows to an ever-expanding virtual realm. These devices are not merely tools but repositories of personal data, gateways to sensitive information, and conduits for communication. The convergence of personal and professional activities within these devices underscores the importance of robust cybersecurity practices. This section delves into the best practices for securing computers, smartphones, and tablets, unraveling the nuances of protection, the threats faced, and the strategies to fortify our digital arsenals.

The foundation of device security is built upon the principles of the CIA Triad—Confidentiality, Integrity, and Availability. These principles guide our approach to protecting data, preventing unauthorized access, and ensuring the continuous functionality of our devices. Central to this foundation is regular software updating. Operating systems and applications often release updates that patch security vulnerabilities, making them less susceptible to exploitation. Neglecting these updates leaves devices vulnerable to known attacks, a lesson painfully demonstrated by major malware outbreaks that exploited unpatched systems.

User authentication and access control are the first defense against unauthorized access. Strong and unique passwords, complemented by multi-factor authentication (MFA), significantly bolster device security. MFA adds a further layer of protection by requiring users to provide multiple verification forms before gaining access. Biometric authentication, like the fingerprint recognition or facial scanning, offers convenience without compromising security. These measures restrict unauthorized users from gaining control over devices and the sensitive data they hold.

Secure browsing habits are paramount for protecting devices from online threats. This includes avoiding suspicious websites, not clicking on unverified links, and being cautious when downloading files or attachments. Adhering to a "least privilege" approach, where apps are granted only the necessary permissions, limits potential risks posed by malicious or poorly designed applications. App stores act as gatekeepers, but even these platforms can be infiltrated by malicious apps. Users should verify app permissions and read reviews before downloading.

Encryption transforms data into an unreadable format, protecting it from unauthorized access. Enabling device encryption adds an extra layer of protection, ensuring that even if a device is lost or stolen, the data remains inaccessible without the decryption key. In parallel, regular data backups are essential. In the face of malware attacks, device failures, or accidental deletion, backups ensure that important data can be restored. Cloud storage and external hard drives provide secure backup options.

Smartphones and tablets are portable repositories of personal and professional information, making their security paramount. Securing these devices Alongside the aforementioned practices involves enabling remote tracking and wiping features. Remote wiping erases data to prevent unauthorized access in case of loss or theft.

Privacy settings, such as location services and app permissions, should be carefully configured to prevent excessive data sharing. Furthermore, disabling unnecessary features like Bluetooth and Wi-Fi when not in use reduces potential attack vectors.

The threats that computers, smartphones, and tablets face are diverse and ever-evolving. Malware, phishing attacks, and ransomware target all types of devices, exploiting vulnerabilities to compromise data or gain unauthorized access. With their vast array of sensors and communication channels, mobile devices are susceptible to location tracking and data leakage. With the advent of the Internet of Things (IoT), devices beyond computers and smartphones—such as smart home devices and wearables—introduce new attack challenges and vectors.

At the core of device security lies education and awareness. Keeping users informed about current threats, attack methods, and best practices is essential. Regular training sessions, whether for individuals or organizations, equip users with the knowledge to recognize and respond to threats. Informed users are less likely to be a victim to scams or inadvertently expose their devices to risks.

In conclusion, securing computers, smartphones, and tablets is not a one-time endeavor; it's a continuous commitment to vigilance and proactive defense. The digital realm is replete with threats, waiting to exploit vulnerabilities and compromise our data. By adopting the best practices outlined here, users can transform their devices from potential gateways for cyber threats into fortified bastions of security. In this dynamic landscape, where personal and professional lives intertwine within the digital sphere, the mastery of device security becomes a critical skill, safeguarding our digital identities and preserving the integrity of our data.

Importance of regular software updates

In the sprawling landscape of the digital age, where our lives are more and more intertwined with technology, the necessity of keeping our devices and software up to date cannot be overstated. The realm of software updates, often overlooked or postponed, serves as a cornerstone of maintaining our digital ecosystem's stability, functionality, and security. This section delves into the paramount importance of regular software updates, uncovering the multifaceted benefits they offer, the vulnerabilities they address, and the implications of neglecting this critical practice.

Software, the lifeblood of our digital existence, is in a constant state of evolution. Developers and engineers continuously work to improve their creations' functionality, user experience, and security. Software updates represent a crucial channel for delivering these improvements to end-users. These updates encompass a spectrum of enhancements, ranging from bug fixes and performance optimizations to the introduction of new features and security patches. Software updates manifest the commitment to ongoing improvement and adaptation to the evolving technological landscape.

One of the most compelling reasons for embracing software updates is their critical role in shoring up our digital defenses. Cyber threats, ranging from malware and viruses to hacking attempts, exploit vulnerabilities in software to gain unauthorized access or compromise data. Security vulnerabilities are often discovered after a software's initial release, making early adopters susceptible to attacks. Security patches, released through updates, plug these vulnerabilities and bolster the software's immunity against malicious actors. The infamous WannaCry ransomware attack of 2017, which targeted systems lacking a crucial security update, is a stark reminder of the consequences of neglecting software updates.

Software updates are not solely about security; they also enrich the functionality and user experience. New features, enhancements, and optimizations are often introduced to meet evolving user needs and technological trends. These updates reflect a software's capacity to remain relevant and responsive to changing demands. By staying current with updates, users ensure they are equipped with the latest tools, features, and capabilities, enhancing their productivity and satisfaction.

The stability and performance of software can degrade over time due to bugs, glitches, and inefficiencies. Regular updates address these issues, providing fixes that restore the software's intended functionality. Performance optimizations can lead to faster load times, smoother user interactions, and improved overall efficiency. Users who opt to delay or skip updates may inadvertently subject themselves to subpar experiences, such as slow responsiveness or unexpected crashes, which hinder their ability to leverage the software's full potential.

Regular software updates are important, but the practice is not without challenges. The convenience of avoiding updates is often driven by the disruption they can cause. Updates may require a system restart, necessitate time for installation, or introduce changes that users must adapt to. In organizational settings, coordinating updates across numerous devices and software instances can be complex. Balancing user convenience and security can be achieved through effective communication, automated updates, and educating users about the benefits of staying current.

Neglecting regular software updates can set off a cascade of negative consequences. Unaddressed vulnerabilities can expose users to data breaches, identity theft, and financial losses. Outdated software may not be compatible with new technologies or interoperable with other software, impeding users' ability to engage effectively in the digital landscape. Moreover, the longer updates are deferred, the more challenging it becomes to integrate them seamlessly, potentially leading to disruptions or conflicts down the line.

In pursuing a secure and technologically advanced digital realm, embracing a proactive maintenance culture is imperative. Regular software updates should be viewed as a responsibility rather than an inconvenience. Organizations and individuals alike must recognize that maintaining software is not an isolated task but an ongoing commitment to the integrity and security of their digital environment.

In conclusion, the significance of regular software updates reverberates across the interconnected digital landscape. Security, functionality, stability, and user experience are intertwined within this practice. Software developers invest substantial efforts in creating and refining their products, and updates represent the culmination of those endeavors. By promptly applying updates, users contribute to a more secure, efficient, and responsive digital world. Neglecting this practice exposes us to avoidable risks and compromises our ability to harness the full potential of technology. The journey to a more resilient digital future begins with a simple act—embracing the power of regular software updates.

Implementing strong passwords and two-factor authentication

In an age where the digital realm permeates every facet of our lives, protecting our online identities has become paramount. Our digital footprints expand as we navigate the virtual landscape, leaving traces of personal, financial, and sensitive information. The twin pillars of strong passwords and two-factor authentication (2FA) emerge as essential tools in safeguarding our digital identities. This section delves into the intricacies of implementing strong passwords and 2FA, exploring their significance, mechanisms, and the collective impact they wield in the fight against cyber threats.

Strong passwords are the first line of defense against unauthorized access to our online accounts. They serve as digital keys that lock the doors to our virtual worlds, safeguarding sensitive information from malicious actors. The anatomy of a strong password involves a blend of complexity, uniqueness, and length. Complex passwords incorporate a mix of upper and lower-case letters, numbers, and special characters. Uniqueness ensures that passwords for different accounts are not reused, preventing the domino effect of a single breach compromising multiple accounts. Length, often overlooked, contributes significantly to a password's strength; longer passwords are exponentially more resilient to brute-force attacks.

Two-factor authentication (2FA) elevates the security paradigm by introducing an additional layer of verification beyond the password. It requires users to provide a second form of verification, typically something they possess, know, or are. The most common 2FA methods include receiving a one-time code via text message, using a hardware token, or utilizing a mobile app. This approach combats the inherent vulnerabilities of passwords, such as theft, phishing, and weak password habits. Even if a password is compromised, the absence of the second verification factor renders unauthorized access futile.

Strong passwords and 2FA constitute a delicate balance between security and convenience. On one hand, complex passwords and multiple verification steps deter attackers, adding layers of difficulty to unauthorized access attempts. On the other hand, user convenience remains a critical consideration. Striking the proper equilibrium entails fostering security practices that users can adopt without impeding their ability to navigate the digital landscape seamlessly.

Despite the importance of strong passwords, the burden of managing multiple complex passwords across various platforms can be overwhelming. Password managers offer a solution by securely storing and auto-filling passwords. These tools alleviate the need for users to memorize a myriad of complex passwords while ensuring that each account has a unique and strong password. However, relying solely on a password manager may introduce a single point of failure; compromising the master password potentially grants access to all stored passwords.

While strong passwords and 2FA are robust defenses, they are not without vulnerabilities. Passwords can be forgotten, leading to frustration and the potential for account lockouts. Users may resort to writing down passwords, which undermines security. Additionally, 2FA methods that rely on text messages can be susceptible to SIM swapping attacks, where attackers hijack a victim's phone number. Biometric 2FA methods, such as fingerprint recognition, raise privacy concerns about data storage and potential misuse.

The human element is a critical factor in implementing strong passwords and 2FA. Education and awareness campaigns are vital in promoting cybersecurity hygiene. Users must be educated about the risks of weak passwords, password reuse, and the importance of 2FA. This includes understanding phishing techniques and social engineering tactics that seek to trick users into revealing their passwords or 2FA codes.

In the grand tapestry of cybersecurity, strong passwords and 2FA are not standalone measures; they are threads woven into a larger defense strategy. Regular software updates, secure browsing habits, and device encryption complement these practices. Organizations and service providers also play a role; implementing security measures, such as rate limiting failed login attempts and monitoring for suspicious activity, can further bolster user protection.

In conclusion, the quest to protect our digital identities is an ongoing endeavor that requires a comprehensive approach. Strong passwords and 2FA emerge as essential components of this strategy, arming users with tools to safeguard their online presence. The threat landscape is ever-evolving, and attackers continuously innovate new methods to breach defenses. By embracing the principles of strong passwords and 2FA, users contribute to a collective effort to create a more secure digital realm—one where the doors to our virtual worlds are fortified against intrusion, and our online identities remain our own.

CHAPTER IV

Safe Internet Practices

Recognizing phishing emails and websites

In the huge expanse of the digital landscape, where communication and transactions unfold seamlessly across virtual realms, the menace of phishing emerges as a shadowy threat. Phishing—similar to a digital con—targets human vulnerability rather than exploiting technical weaknesses. The deceptive art of crafting emails and websites masquerading as legitimate entities has proven lucrative for cybercriminals seeking to steal personal information, credentials, and financial resources. This section delves into the intricate world of phishing, unraveling its techniques, exploring its consequences, and offering insights into recognizing phishing emails and websites, empowering users to navigate this treacherous terrain.

Phishing, the digital equivalent of a baited trap, thrives on exploiting human psychology rather than relying solely on technical vulnerabilities. Cybercriminals impersonate trusted entities—often financial institutions, email service providers, or e-commerce platforms—enticing recipients into divulging sensitive information. Spear phishing, a targeted variant, tailors messages to specific individuals, amplifying the illusion of authenticity. Whaling, another form, targets high-profile individuals or executives. Vishing and smishing, employing voice calls and SMS respectively, extend the reach of phishing to voice and text communication channels.

Phishing emails and websites are meticulously crafted to deceive even the most discerning recipients. Emails typically employ techniques such as urgency, fear, or promises of rewards to prompt recipients to take hasty actions. URLs may appear legitimate at first glance, but subtle variations or misspellings often reveal their true nature. Hyperlinks can be cloaked, redirecting users to malicious websites. Similar to authentic counterparts down to the logos and branding, websites coax users into entering personal information, credentials, or financial details.

Vigilance is the armor against phishing attacks. Users must be attuned to the telltale signs distinguishing phishing emails and websites from legitimate communications. Misspelled or distorted URLs, generic salutations, and poorly constructed content indicate phishing attempts. Urgent or threatening language that generates a sense of panic warrants skepticism. Requests for sensitive information, especially passwords or financial details, should be met with caution. Hovering over hyperlinks without clicking can reveal the actual destination URL, aiding in identification.

Recognizing phishing emails and websites hinges on educating users about the tactics employed by cybercriminals. Regular training sessions, whether for individuals or organizations, equip users with the knowledge to determine and respond to phishing attempts. Simulated phishing exercises can provide real-world practice in spotting malicious emails. Beyond formal training, fostering a culture of skepticism and encouraging users to verify requests via alternate communication channels can further fortify defenses.

The consequences of falling prey to phishing can be dire, ranging from financial loss to identity theft. Stolen credentials grant cybercriminals access to personal accounts, which they can exploit for financial gain or to launch further attacks. Ransomware attacks, where malware encrypts data and demands payment for its release, can be triggered through phishing links or attachments. Phishing incidents can tarnish an individual's reputation, compromise sensitive business information, and erode trust in digital communication platforms.

Phishing tactics are ever-evolving, adapting to technological advancements and user behaviors. Smishing and vishing attacks exploit communication channels beyond email, targeting users through voice and text messages. Phishing campaigns capitalize on current events, leveraging public concerns to create urgency and elicit responses. Impersonation of trusted entities extends to social media, where cyber criminals create fake profiles to establish credibility and deceive users.

Recognizing phishing emails and websites necessitates a multifaceted approach. Technological solutions, such as email filters that identify and quarantine phishing emails, provide a layer of defense. Web browsers and security software often include features that flag potentially malicious websites. User behaviors, such as verifying sender identities, scrutinizing URLs, and hesitating before acting on urgent requests, reinforce these technical defenses.

In conclusion, recognizing phishing emails and websites is not merely a skill—it's a survival instinct in the digital age. The complexity and adaptability of phishing tactics demand that users remain vigilant and informed. As the virtual landscape continues evolving, so too do the threats assail it. By arming ourselves with knowledge, skepticism, and the ability to discern between authentic communication and deceptive ploys, we empower ourselves to navigate the treacherous waters of the digital realm, safeguarding our identities, assets, and the integrity of our online interactions.

Using secure and private browsing

In the digital age, where the internet serves as a vast repository of information, communication, and commerce, the pursuit of online privacy has become a pressing concern. Individuals' actions and interactions are increasingly scrutinized, recorded, and exploited as they traverse the virtual realm. Amidst this surveillance and data collection landscape, the concept of secure and private browsing emerges as a beacon of hope. This section delves into the realm of secure and private browsing, unraveling its significance, mechanics, and implications for safeguarding online identities and preserving personal data.

The dawn of the internet brought an open and interconnected space, but this very openness led to concerns about privacy and security. Traditional web browsing exposes users to many risks, from tracking cookies that record online behavior to malicious actors exploiting vulnerabilities in browser software. As awareness of these threats grew, the demand for secure and private browsing solutions gained momentum, setting the stage for the evolution of browsing practices.

Secure and private browsing represents a departure from conventional browsing practices. Secure browsing protects users from online threats and malware by employing encryption, secure protocols, and anti-tracking measures. Private browsing, on the other hand, centers on preserving user anonymity and data privacy. It prevents storing browsing history, cookies, and temporary files, ensuring that no traces of online activities persist on the user's device.

Encryption stands as a cornerstone of secure and private browsing. Secure Sockets Layer (SSL) as well as Transport Layer Security (TLS) protocols encrypt data exchanged between the user's device and the website, thwarting eavesdropping attempts. This encryption safeguards sensitive information, such as login credentials and financial transactions, from interception and exploitation. Users can identify encrypted connections through a padlock icon in the browser's address bar.

Tracking mechanisms, often employed by advertisers and data collectors, monitor online behavior to build user profiles and deliver targeted advertisements. Secure and private browsing solutions incorporate anti-tracking measures to prevent these trackers from recording user activities. Enhanced Tracking Protection (ETP) in some browsers blocks known trackers, limiting the amount of data collected about users' online habits.

Virtual Private Networks (VPNs) and proxies offer additional security and privacy. By routing internet traffic through servers in different geographic locations, VPNs and proxies mask users' IP addresses, making it difficult to trace their online activities back to them. This technique not only enhances privacy but also circumvents geographic restrictions and censorship.

Most modern browsers offer private browsing modes that prevent the storage of browsing history, cookies, and other temporary files. These modes, often called "Incognito" or "Private" modes, provide a degree of anonymity by isolating the browsing session from the user's regular browsing data. However, it's important to note that private browsing doesn't offer complete anonymity; ISPs, websites, and other entities may still gather some information.

While secure and private browsing is a powerful tool, it has challenges and limitations. Not all websites support encryption, potentially exposing users to unsecured connections. VPNs and proxies, while effective, can introduce latency and impact browsing speed. Advertisers and data collectors continuously adapt to anti-tracking measures, creating a cat-and-mouse game between privacy advocates and those seeking to exploit user data.

A delicate balance exists between convenience and privacy in the realm of secure and private browsing. Some privacy-enhancing measures, such as disabling cookies or scripts, may affect the functionality of certain websites. Users must decide how much they're willing to trade off convenience for privacy. The advent of privacy-focused browsers and browser extensions offers users more control over their online experiences.

Secure and private browsing is part of a broader movement advocating digital privacy and autonomy. It aligns with conversations surrounding data protection regulations, user consent, and the ethical collection of personal information. Using secure and private browsing tools is a testament to individuals asserting control over their digital footprint and demanding greater transparency from the entities that collect their data.

In conclusion, secure and private browsing transcends mere technical practices; it embodies the aspiration for control over one's online identity. In a landscape marked by constant data collection and the erosion of privacy, secure and private browsing solutions emerge as beacons of hope, offering users the tools to shield their actions, communications, and personal data from prying eyes. By embracing these practices, users contribute to a collective effort to reclaim a measure of autonomy in the digital realm—where privacy is a fundamental right rather than a mere afterthought.

Safe social media usage and privacy settings

The digital era has ushered in a paradigm shift in how we connect, communicate, and share our lives. Social media platforms, the virtual town squares of our time, have become integral to the fabric of modern society. Yet, within the realms of status updates, likes, and hashtags, the delicate balance between connectivity and privacy often teeters on the edge. Safe social media usage and privacy settings emerge as the linchpin of our digital interactions, offering a means to safeguard personal information and maintain control over our virtual identities. This section delves into the multifaceted world of social media privacy, exploring its nuances, the implications of oversharing, and the art of crafting robust privacy settings to navigate the complexities of the digital social landscape.

With its promise of instantaneous connection and global reach, social media has transformed how we communicate and share. It has democratized information dissemination, empowered social movements, and facilitated global conversations. However, the captivating allure of social media can mask its potential pitfalls. Oversharing, the unbridled disclosure of personal information, exposes users to privacy breaches, identity theft, and even physical risks. The boundary between the digital and physical world blurs as location tags, check-ins, and personal details intertwine, inviting unintended consequences.

Privacy settings, the digital equivalents of virtual barriers, enable individuals or users to control who can access their content, interact with them, and view their personal information. They provide the tools to curate digital experiences that align with individual preferences and comfort levels. These settings encompass a range of controls, from determining who can see posts and profile information to regulating friend requests and blocking users. Privacy settings vary between platforms, but they are designed to give users agency over their online interactions.

Safe social media usage begins with crafting a digital persona that reflects authenticity and discretion. Users must evaluate the information they choose to share, bearing in mind the potential reach of their content. Birthdays, phone numbers, addresses, and other sensitive information should be cautiously approached. Auditing friends or connections can help minimize the risk of sharing personal details with strangers. The posts we share contribute to our digital footprint, leaving indelible traces of our lives; as such, the decision to share should be guided by mindfulness.

Privacy settings offer the ability to segment your audience, ensuring that content reaches only the intended recipients. Public posts are visible to anyone, while friends-only or custom lists allow users to restrict access to specific individuals or groups. This segmentation empowers users to share personal updates with close friends and family while maintaining a more public-facing presence for professional networking or community engagement.

Social media platforms often allow users to control who can tag them in a posts, photos, and comments. Enabling review options ensures that tags are only visible after user approval. This feature prevents the unwarranted association with content that may not align with one's digital persona. Additionally, users can restrict the ability of friends or connections to post directly on their timeline, reducing the likelihood of unwanted or irrelevant content.

The rise of location-sharing features on social media platforms adds a new layer of complexity to privacy considerations. While sharing your location can enhance the real-time nature of interactions, it can also reveal your physical whereabouts to a broader audience. Disabling location services for specific apps or posts, or sharing your location only with a select group of friends, helps strike a balance between social engagement and personal safety.

Balancing sharing and privacy is a nuanced endeavor. While stringent privacy settings can fortify your online security, excessively restrictive settings might hinder your ability to engage and connect with others. A thoughtful approach involves periodic review and adjustment of privacy settings as social media platforms evolve and user preferences change. Users should remain aware of changes in platform policies that could affect their privacy settings or the visibility of their content.

Educating users about safe social media usage and privacy settings is essential. Schools, organizations, and community groups can conduct workshops to raise awareness about the risks of oversharing and the benefits of proactive privacy management. Encouraging users to regularly review their privacy settings, update passwords, and enable two-factor authentication can empower them to take control of their digital presence.

As technology improves and the digital landscape evolves, the landscape of social media privacy will continue to transform. New features and challenges will emerge, necessitating ongoing awareness and adaptation. The ethical use of data by social media platforms will remain a topic of debate, driving conversations about user consent, data ownership, and regulatory frameworks.

In conclusion, the realm of safe social media usage and privacy settings is a dynamic tapestry woven from threads of digital empowerment and personal responsibility. As we navigate the virtual town squares of social media platforms, we are tasked with preserving the delicate balance between connectivity and privacy. By embracing privacy settings, understanding the implications of oversharing, and fostering a culture of awareness, users can confidently navigate the digital social landscape, ensuring that their online interactions align with their values and aspirations. In this landscape of perpetual connection, the mastery of privacy becomes an essential skill, shielding our digital identities and preserving the sanctity of our personal space amidst the bustling digital crowds.

CHAPTER V

Data Protection Measures

Importance of data backup and recovery strategies

In the intricate web of the digital age, where every keystroke and click leaves an indelible mark, the value of data transcends mere information—it embodies the essence of our personal, professional, and creative endeavors. Yet, the digital realm is not impervious to the capricious forces of data loss, whether due to hardware failures, cyber attacks, or human error. Against this backdrop, the significance of data backup and recovery strategies comes to the forefront as a beacon of resilience in the face of adversity. This section delves into the intricate tapestry of data backup and recovery, exploring its multifaceted importance, the methods and strategies at its core, and the implications of a world where data's impermanence goes unchecked.

Data, in its myriad forms, fuels the engines of the modern world. From personal memories captured in photos and videos to critical business documents, databases, and intellectual property, data underpins our digital interactions. Its loss can have far-reaching consequences, eroding the foundations of personal identity, disrupting business continuity, and extinguishing the fruits of innovation. The digital era's reliance on data transforms it into a currency that demands safeguarding against the myriad perils that threaten its existence.

Data backup, the art of preserving digital landscapes, involves the creation of duplicate copies of critical information. This practice guards against data loss by establishing redundancies that can be accessed during a primary copy's compromise. The science of data backup encompasses a range of methods, from local backups stored on physical devices to remote backups on cloud platforms. The choice of method depends on data volume, accessibility requirements, and the desired level of protection.

The advent of cloud technology has revolutionized data backup and recovery. Cloud backup involves storing data on remote servers hosted by service providers. This approach offers benefits such as scalability, accessibility from anywhere with an internet connection, and automated backup processes. The cloud's distributed nature enhances data redundancy, mitigating risks associated with localized failures. Additionally, cloud backup streamlines recovery processes, allowing users to restore data swiftly after an incident.

Data loss can occur because of many factors, with human error and cyber threats standing as prominent adversaries. Accidental deletion, data corruption, or mismanagement can all lead to irrevocable loss. Cyber threats, from malware and ransomware attacks to hacking and phishing, target data's integrity and availability. Recovery strategies must account for these multifaceted risks, offering mechanisms to restore data to its original state before the incident occurred.

Data backup is not a standalone endeavor—it's intrinsically linked to recovery strategies. A comprehensive recovery strategy outlines the steps to be taken in case of data loss or compromise. This includes identifying critical data, setting recovery point objectives (or RPOs) and recovery time objectives (or RTOs), and establishing protocols for initiating and executing recovery processes. A well-defined recovery strategy ensures that data is restored promptly, minimizing disruptions and mitigating the impact of data loss.

For businesses, data backup and recovery strategies are indispensable components of business continuity and disaster recovery plans. These plans outline how an organization will operate and recover in the face of disruptions, ensuring minimal downtime and maintaining customer trust. Data backup and recovery strategies are integral to these plans, acting as lifeboats that keep organizations afloat when turbulent waters threaten to capsize their operations.

The economic ramifications of data loss are profound. For businesses, downtime resulting from data loss translates into lost revenue, diminished productivity, and reputational damage. The costs associated with data recovery efforts, potential legal liabilities, and fines for non-compliance with data protection regulations further compound the financial toll. On a personal level, data loss can lead to emotional distress, loss of cherished memories, and disruptions to daily life.

Data's impermanence beckons the need for a paradigm shift—an understanding that its preservation requires proactive measures. Organizations must invest in robust data backup and recovery strategies, backed by regular testing and refinement. Individuals, too, can harness the power of technology to safeguard their digital footprints. Automated backup solutions, combined with adherence to secure browsing and cybersecurity best practices, form a holistic approach to data preservation.

In a world where data is both the lifeblood and Achilles' heel of the digital era, the importance of data backup and recovery strategies looms large. These strategies transcend mere technical practices; they embody the resilience of individuals, businesses, and societies against the unrelenting tide of data loss. By embracing data backup and recovery, users assert control over their digital destinies, arming themselves with the tools to defy the impermanence that threatens their digital legacies. In the realm where past, present, and future intertwine, data backup and recovery strategies emerge as a force of preservation—a testament to the indomitable spirit of human endeavor in the face of uncertainty.

Exploring cloud storage security

In the digital age, where data's ubiquity shapes our personal and professional landscapes, the emergence of cloud storage has transformed how we store, access, and share information. The allure of seamless synchronization, accessibility from anywhere, and virtually limitless storage capacity has propelled cloud storage into the mainstream. Yet, this technological leap forward is not without its shadows—cloud storage security emerges as a critical consideration in an era of cyber threats and data breaches. This section delves into the multifaceted world of cloud storage security, unraveling its complexities, delving into the shared responsibility model, exploring encryption practices, and examining the role of user awareness in safeguarding the digital realm's ethereal vaults.

The shift from local storage to cloud storage is similar to an evolution—expanding possibilities and conveniences. Traditional local storage relied on physical devices like hard drives and USBs, tethering data to a single location. On the other hand, cloud storage liberates data from these constraints, enabling seamless access from many devices and locations. However, this newfound freedom comes with a price—the potential for data breaches, unauthorized access, and loss looms large, underscoring the imperative of robust security measures.

Cloud storage security is not solely the responsibility of service providers—it's a shared endeavor. The shared responsibility model delineates the division of security responsibilities between cloud service providers and users. Providers secure the underlying infrastructure and services, ensuring data center protection, network security, and hardware maintenance. Users, in turn, are responsible for securing the data they store in the cloud, employing encryption, setting access controls, and adhering to best practices in user authentication.

Encryption, the act of encoding data to prevent unauthorized access, stands as a sentinel guarding the sanctity of information stored in the cloud. End-to-end encryption ensures that data remains confidential even when transmitted to and from the cloud. While at rest in the cloud, data encryption ensures that it remains unintelligible to anyone without the necessary decryption keys. Encryption's role in cloud storage security is paramount; it thwarts eavesdropping attempts and mitigates the risk of data breaches resulting from unauthorized access.

Access controls, the digital gateways that regulate who can access data, are pivotal in cloud storage security. Users must configure access controls meticulously, defining who can view, edit, or delete their stored content. The principle of least privilege guides these settings—granting users only the permissions necessary for their tasks. Regularly reviewing and adjusting access controls as roles and responsibilities change prevents unauthorized access and minimizes the risk of data leakage.

Multi-factor authentication, also known as MFA, is an additional layer of security beyond passwords, fortifies cloud storage accounts against unauthorized access. MFA requires users to provide a second verification factor, often something they possess, know, or are, before gaining access. This approach mitigates the risk of compromised passwords, which can lead to data breaches. MFA methods include one-time codes sent to mobile devices, biometric recognition, and hardware tokens.

The human element is central to cloud storage security. User awareness, education, and adherence to best practices are pivotal in mitigating risks. Users must be informed about phishing attacks, social engineering tactics, and the importance of strong, unique passwords. Regular training and simulations can simulate real-world cyber threats, equipping users with the skills to identify and respond effectively.

Cloud storage transcends geographical borders, raising questions about regulatory compliance and data sovereignty. Organizations must ensure that the cloud service provider complies with data protection regulations relevant to their jurisdiction. Data sovereignty, the notion that data is subject to the laws of the country in which it is stored, adds layer of complexity. Organizations must choose cloud providers that align with their compliance requirements.

Selecting a reputable and secure cloud service provider is a critical step in cloud storage security. Vendor risk management involves assessing the provider's security practices, data protection measures, and adherence to industry standards. Evaluating the provider's history of security incidents, their response to breaches, and their data recovery protocols is essential in making an informed decision.

Cloud storage security assumes paramount importance in a landscape where the boundaries of physical and digital realms blur. Data breaches and cyber attacks underscore the fragility of the digital vaults that house our information. By embracing a culture of vigilance, informed decision-making, and proactive security measures, users and organizations can confidently navigate the cloud's vast expanse. Cloud storage security is not an isolated task—it's a collective endeavor that bridges technological prowess with human awareness, forging a fortified barrier against the perils that threaten to compromise the digital realm's ethereal vaults.

In conclusion, the landscape of cloud storage security extends beyond the confines of technology—it's an intricate tapestry woven from shared responsibilities, encryption fortresses, access controls, and user awareness. Cloud storage, while a testament to the digital era's innovation, remains susceptible to the turbulence of the virtual realm. By understanding the nuances of cloud storage security, users, organizations, and society at large can harness the power of technology while safeguarding their digital assets against the ever-evolving threats that lurk in the shadows. The journey through the cloud's nebulous corridors is not without its challenges, but with the suitable safeguards in place, it becomes a voyage of empowerment—a journey where data's integrity and confidentiality remain steadfast amidst the ebb and flow of the digital tide.

Data retention policies and data disposal practices

In the intricate tapestry of the digital age, data assumes the role of a digital memory—a repository of knowledge, experiences, and interactions that shape the contours of our lives. As the volume of data generated and stored grows exponentially, managing and safeguarding this digital legacy becomes paramount. Data retention policies and disposal practices emerge as the guardians of this legacy, dictating the lifespan of data and the mechanisms through which it is preserved or purged. This section delves into the multifaceted realm of data retention and disposal, exploring the importance of structured policies, the implications of unchecked data accumulation, and the ethical considerations that underpin responsible data stewardship.

Data retention, the practice of storing data for a defined period, is a cornerstone of modern information management. It encompasses a spectrum of data types, from business records and personal communications to financial transactions and research findings. Data retention policies outline the guidelines for determining how long data should be retained based on legal requirements, business needs, and historical significance. These policies ensure that organizations and individuals maintain a structured approach to data preservation, steering clear of the pitfalls of data hoarding.

The intersection of data retention and privacy is a delicate balance. While data retention serves essential purposes such as compliance with regulations, legal discovery, and historical record-keeping, it also raises concerns about individuals' privacy rights. Retaining personal data beyond its necessary lifespan increases the risk of unauthorized access, breaches of data, and potential exploitation. Striking a balance requires defining clear retention periods, anonymizing or pseudonymizing data when possible, and adhering to data protection principles prioritizing data subjects' rights.

Data retention policies are intrinsically tied to the regulatory landscape. Different jurisdictions and industries impose varying requirements for data retention periods. Organizations must navigate the complexity of regulations, including data protection rules like the General Data Protection Regulation, also known as GDPR, of the European Union and industry-specific mandates like the Health Insurance Portability and Accountability Act (HIPAA). Compliance with these regulations necessitates aligning data retention policies with legal requirements, which can vary from a few months to several years.

Beyond regulatory compliance, business needs and historical significance influence data retention policies. Businesses must evaluate the value of data for decision-making, customer service, and analytics. Customer records, financial transactions, and communications archives often have more extended retention periods to support ongoing operations and legal inquiries. Similarly, historical significance drives the retention of cultural, scientific, and archival data, ensuring that knowledge is preserved for future generations.

Just as data retention ensures that data is preserved when necessary, data disposal ensures that data is discarded when its retention period expires. Data disposal practices encompass a range of techniques, from physical destruction of hardware to secure data erasure and software-driven deletion. Secure data disposal mitigates the risk of unauthorized data recovery, protecting against data breaches and leaks resulting from discarded equipment or storage media.

Secure data erasure, a systematic process that renders data unreadable and irrecoverable, is pivotal in data disposal. This process involves overwriting data with random patterns multiple times, effectively obliterating the original content. Secure data erasure applies to various storage media, including hard drives, solid-state drives, and mobile devices. Implementing secure data erasure before repurposing, selling, or discarding hardware prevents the accidental exposure of sensitive information.

In the era of cloud storage, data disposal extends beyond physical media to encompass virtual spaces. Cloud service providers must adhere to rigorous data disposal practices to remove data remnants from previous users before new tenants utilize the same resources. For users, the migration or termination of cloud services demands careful consideration of data disposal, as residual data may persist if not appropriately managed.

Data retention and disposal practices are underpinned by ethical considerations that extend beyond legal mandates. Data stewards must ask themselves whether retaining data is ethically justifiable, considering factors like consent, potential harm, and the principle of proportionality. The concept of digital legacy—that future generations will inherit the digital footprints of the present—raises questions about the permanence of data and the implications of data disposal decisions on posterity.

Data disposal practices also intersect with environmental responsibility. E-waste from discarded electronic equipment poses ecological hazards due to toxic components and inefficient recycling processes. Responsible data disposal includes partnering with certified e-waste recyclers and adopting sustainable practices that minimize the ecological impact of electronic device disposal.

In conclusion, the landscape of data retention policies and data disposal practices is a testament to the evolving relationship between humans and their digital legacy. The responsible stewardship of data encompasses the art of preservation, the science of deletion, and the ethical considerations guiding decisions about what to retain and release. By embracing structured data retention policies, adhering to legal and regulatory mandates, and implementing secure data disposal practices, individuals and organizations navigate the digital realm with integrity, safeguarding sensitive information, respecting privacy rights, and shaping a legacy that resonates with the values of responsible data stewardship. In the ever-evolving chronicle of human history, the guardianship of data—both in its preservation and eventual farewell—becomes an integral chapter in the narrative of our digital existence.

CHAPTER VI

Network Security

Understanding firewalls and intrusion detection/prevention systems

In the intricate realm of the digital landscape, where information flows ceaselessly and virtual worlds intertwine with reality, the specter of cyber threats looms large. As the borders between the physical and digital worlds blur, the need to fortify the digital perimeter becomes paramount. Firewalls and Intrusion Detection/Prevention Systems, or IDS/IPS, emerge as the digital sentinels guarding against unauthorized access, malicious attacks, and data breaches. This section delves into the intricate world of firewalls and IDS/IPS, unraveling their roles, mechanisms, the evolving threat landscape they combat, and the symbiotic relationship that underpins their collective role in fortifying the citadel of digital security.

Firewalls are the guardians of the digital threshold—a barrier that separates the realms of trusted and untrusted networks. Functioning as a gatekeeper, a firewall scrutinizes incoming and outgoing network traffic, permitting or denying passage based on predefined security rules. It operates at various network stack layers, from the traditional network layer to the more granular application layer. By filtering traffic based on IP addresses, port numbers, and application protocols, firewalls mitigate the risk of unauthorized access, malware infiltration, and the exploitation of vulnerabilities.

Firewalls manifest in diverse forms, each tailored to the nuances of modern network architectures. Network-based firewalls are situated at the perimeter of a network, safeguarding all incoming and outgoing traffic. On the other hand, host-based firewalls reside on individual devices, exerting control over traffic specific to that device. Next-generation firewalls combine traditional filtering with deep packet inspection, application identification, and intrusion prevention capabilities. Firewalls can be deployed as hardware appliances, software applications, or virtual instances, adapting to the dynamic needs of organizations' digital infrastructures.

The evolution of cyber threats demands a proactive approach to digital security. Intrusion Detection Systems (or IDS) and Intrusion Prevention Systems (or IPS) are pivotal in this endeavor. IDS observes network traffic for suspicious activity and strange patterns, flagging potential threats for further investigation. IPS, a more assertive counterpart, not only detects but also takes preventive action by blocking or quarantining suspicious traffic in real-time. IDS and IPS are armed with signature-based detection, behavioral analysis, and anomaly detection mechanisms to counteract emerging threats.

The inception of Machine Learning as well as Artificial Intelligence has redefined the capabilities of firewalls and IDS/IPS. AI-driven systems can analyze vast datasets, identifying patterns that might elude human scrutiny. ML algorithms, trained on historical attack data, enable adaptive threat detection by recognizing new attack vectors and unknown threats. This symbiotic integration of human expertise and machine intelligence equips security systems to anticipate, identify, and respond to threats more accurately and efficiently.

While AI and ML augment threat detection, the human element remains pivotal in configuring, fine-tuning, and interpreting firewall and IDS/IPS outputs. Security professionals define security policies, whitelist trusted applications, and identify the thresholds for triggering alerts. The careful calibration of these systems ensures that false positives are minimized, genuine threats are promptly addressed, and the digital landscape is not overwhelmed by the cacophony of alarms.

The contemporary threat landscape is characterized by its dynamic nature—attack techniques evolve, exploit vectors shift, and vulnerabilities are unearthed. Threat intelligence, a collaborative effort aggregating and disseminating information about emerging threats, empowers firewalls and IDS/IPS to stay one step ahead. Organizations can subscribe to threat intelligence feeds that provide real-time updates on malicious IP addresses, domain names, and attack indicators. This proactive approach enables security systems to preemptively block potential threats, bolstering the overall resilience of the digital fortress.

While firewalls and IDS/IPS are potent tools, they are not immune to challenges. The complexity of modern network infrastructures, encrypted traffic, and sophisticated attack techniques can occasionally result in false positives—legitimate traffic being flagged as malicious. Balancing robust security with operational efficiency requires constant fine-tuning and adjustments to security policies. Striking this balance ensures that security measures do not inadvertently hinder legitimate activities and communication.

Firewalls and IDS/IPS are integral components of a broader strategy known as defense-in-depth—a multi-layered approach to security that employs various security mechanisms to safeguard against a spectrum of threats. Firewalls and IDS/IPS collaborate with antivirus software, encryption protocols, access controls, and employee training to create a fortified defense ecosystem. This layered approach recognizes that no single security precaution is foolproof and that a combination of defenses is the most effective way to thwart sophisticated attacks.

In the evolving cyber threat landscape, end users are often the first line of defense. Educating users about phishing attacks, social engineering tactics, and secure online behavior is pivotal. Vigilant users can help identify potential threats, report suspicious activities, and prevent security breaches. Training programs, simulated phishing campaigns, and ongoing awareness initiatives empower users to participate actively in the collective effort to safeguard digital assets.

In conclusion, the evolving digital panorama demands dynamic defenses—enter firewalls and IDS/IPS, the vigilant sentinels of the digital realm. These technologies epitomize the synergy of human expertise and technological innovation, offering a multi-dimensional defense against the relentless tide of cyber threats. By understanding their roles, harnessing their capabilities, and embracing collaboration, organizations can confidently navigate the intricate landscape of digital security. The guardians of the digital perimeter stand poised, not merely as reactive responders, but as proactive custodians of the citadel—a bastion that fortifies the digital landscape against the unpredictable forces that seek to breach its walls.

Wireless network security tips

In the era of seamless connectivity, where wireless networks intertwine our digital and physical lives, the allure of untethered access is accompanied by a symphony of security challenges. While liberating users from physical constraints, wireless networks also open avenues for cyber threats, data breaches, and unauthorized access. Against this backdrop, wireless network security emerges as an essential fortress— ensuring that the convenience of wireless connectivity is not undermined by the perils that lurk in the airwaves. This section explores the intricate landscape of wireless network security, delving into the nuances of secure configurations, encryption protocols, guest network management, and the role of user awareness in fortifying the digital airwaves.

Wireless networks have woven themselves into the fabric of modern life, seamlessly bridging the digital and physical realms. The allure of browsing the internet, streaming content, and connecting devices without the constraints of wires is undeniable. However, the very convenience that wireless networks offer comes with a caveat—the increased vulnerability to cyber threats and unauthorized access. The open nature of wireless transmissions allows potential attackers to intercept data, launch man-in-the-middle attacks, and exploit vulnerabilities in poorly secured networks.

Secure configurations form the bedrock of wireless network security. Access points and routers must be set up with robust passwords, disabling default credentials that are easily exploitable. Renaming network identifiers (SSIDs) to avoid broadcasting default names and turning off remote management are essential to limiting potential attack vectors. Additionally, firmware updates—regularly issued by manufacturers—address security vulnerabilities and must be promptly installed to maintain the network's integrity.

Encryption, the process of encoding data to prevent unauthorized access, is paramount for protecting data in transit over wireless networks. WPA3 (Wi-Fi Protected Access 3) is the latest encryption protocol, offering improved security over its predecessors. It utilizes more robust encryption algorithms and introduces features like individualized data encryption for users, thwarting attacks like eavesdropping and packet decryption. Enabling WPA3 and choosing strong encryption passwords are pivotal in ensuring the confidentiality of wireless communications.

Guest networks, a common feature of wireless routers, allow visitors to access the internet without gaining access to the primary network. This segregation mitigates potential risks associated with unauthorized devices or users. Configuring guest networks with separate SSIDs and enabling a password or captive portal for authentication ensures that guests can enjoy connectivity without jeopardizing the security of the main network. Regularly updating guest network passwords further bolsters security.

MAC address filtering offers an additional layer of access control to wireless networks. Every network-enabled device has a unique MAC address, and administrators can allow or deny access based on these addresses. While this method adds some control, it is not foolproof, as MAC addresses can be spoofed. Therefore, MAC address filtering should complement other security measures to prevent unauthorized access.

The human element is a linchpin in wireless network security. Educating users about the risks of connecting to unsecured networks, the importance of strong passwords, and the implications of sharing sensitive information over public Wi-Fi is essential. Users should be cautious about connecting to unknown networks, especially those without passwords or encryption. Encouraging users to turn off automatic network connections and utilize virtual private networks (VPNs) when accessing public Wi-Fi can mitigate risks.

Public Wi-Fi, while a boon for staying connected on the go, presents unique security challenges. Public networks lack the layered security protocols of home networks, making them susceptible to attacks like man-in-the-middle interceptions and session hijacking. When using public Wi-Fi, users should avoid accessing sensitive information, like online banking or email accounts, unless a VPN is employed to encrypt data transmissions. Turning off file sharing and enabling the device's firewall further enhances security.

While digital defenses are paramount, the physical security of devices is often overlooked. Wireless routers and access points should be placed in secure locations, away from windows and readily accessible areas. Restricting physical access to these devices prevents unauthorized tampering and ensures that attackers cannot exploit vulnerabilities by physically interacting with the hardware.

Wireless network security is not a set-and-forget endeavor—it requires regular audits and monitoring. Network administrators should periodically review access logs, identify unusual activity, and promptly investigate and address anomalies. Additionally, periodic vulnerability assessments and penetration testing can identify potential weak points and vulnerabilities that must be addressed to maintain a robust security posture.

In conclusion, wireless network security is a dynamic symphony that harmonizes technology and vigilance. As wireless networks permeate every facet of modern life, the responsibility to fortify the digital airwaves against threats becomes paramount. By adhering to secure configurations, embracing encryption, judiciously managing guest networks, and fostering user awareness, individuals and organizations can confidently navigate the wireless landscape. The guardianship of wireless network security demands constant vigilance, a proactive mindset, and a commitment to staying one step ahead of the adversaries that seek to breach the digital perimeter. In this ethereal arena where bits and bytes traverse the airwaves, the harmony of security and connectivity emerges as the ultimate crescendo—an enduring testament to human ingenuity in the face of evolving cyber challenges.

Virtual Private Networks (VPNs) for secure connections

In the intricate fabric of the digital realm, where information flows ceaselessly and virtual landscapes interweave with reality, the imperative of safeguarding sensitive data and ensuring privacy has never been more vital. As our digital footprints extend across geographies and networks, secure connections are paramount. Enter Virtual Private Networks (VPNs)—digital sanctuaries that cloak online activities, shield sensitive information, and empower users to navigate the digital expanse confidently. This section delves into the complex tapestry of VPNs, unraveling their mechanisms, exploring their benefits, dissecting the various use cases, and highlighting the ethical considerations underpinning their role as sentinels in the digital void.

At its core, a VPN is a secure conduit tunnel through which data travels between a user's device and a remote server. This tunnel is encrypted, rendering data indecipherable to potential eavesdroppers. VPNs extend beyond the protective veil of encryption; they also bestow users with a new IP address, concealing their actual geographic location and making it appear like they are browsing from a different location. This multipronged approach to security and privacy establishes the foundation upon which VPNs operate.

Encryption is the cornerstone of VPNs, the process of converting data into a cipher that can only be deciphered with a corresponding decryption key. The encryption used in VPNs employs robust algorithms that ensure the confidentiality of data as it traverses the often tumultuous highways of the internet. Whether browsing websites, sending emails, or engaging in online transactions, data is shrouded in an impenetrable code, thwarting potential interceptions by cyber adversaries.

VPNs offer a dual gift—privacy and anonymity. VPNs render their online activities virtually untraceable by masking the user's IP address. This safeguards users' personal information and prevents websites, advertisers, and even governments from harvesting data about their online behavior. VPNs empower users to explore the digital realm anonymously, deterring prying eyes from profiling their digital identities.

One of the intriguing facets of VPNs is their ability to geo-spoof—to make it appear that the user is accessing the internet from another location than their actual one. This can be particularly useful for circumventing geo-restrictions imposed by streaming services, websites, or countries. By tunneling through servers located in different parts of the world, VPN users can access content that may be blocked or inaccessible from their actual location.

Public Wi-Fi networks, while convenient, often lack robust security measures. This makes them susceptible to cyber attacks like man-in-the-middle interceptions and session hijacking. VPNs safeguard against these vulnerabilities by encrypting data transmitted over public networks. When connected to a VPN, users can browse the internet, access their email, and engage in online activities without exposing their data to potential snoopers.

In the modern landscape of remote work and distributed teams, VPNs serve as a lifeline for secure remote connections. They enable employees to access corporate networks, files, and resources from remote locations, ensuring that sensitive data remains protected even when traversing public networks. VPNs establish a secure link between the remote worker's device and the corporate network, mitigating the risks associated with remote access.

While VPNs empower individuals to shield their online activities, ethical considerations emerge. VPNs can be used for malicious purposes, such as concealing illegal activities or launching cyber attacks. Striking a balance between privacy and responsibility is paramount. VPN service providers often outline acceptable use policies, prohibiting activities that violate the law or compromise the security of others. It is incumbent upon users to employ VPNs responsibly and adhere to the ethical principles that underpin their use.

Selecting a VPN service provider requires careful consideration. Factors such as the provider's reputation, the level of encryption offered, the number and distribution of server locations, and the availability of dedicated IP addresses must be evaluated. Additionally, user-friendliness, customer support, and compatibility with different devices and operating systems play a pivotal role in determining the suitability of a VPN.

While VPNs offer a robust layer of security and privacy, they are not a panacea. VPNs can slow down internet speeds because of the encryption and routing processes, impacting streaming and online gaming experiences. Moreover, the level of privacy offered by VPNs depends on the provider's logging policy—some may log user data, defeating the purpose of anonymity. Users should conduct thorough research to choose a VPN that aligns with their privacy and security requirements.

In conclusion, the realm of Virtual Private Networks (VPNs) is a realm where security, privacy, and anonymity converge. In a digital landscape where data breaches, surveillance, and cyber threats cast a shadow, VPNs emerge as a beacon—a shield that empowers users to reclaim control over their online experiences. VPNs underscore the importance of secure connections in an interconnected world by leveraging the power of encryption, geo-spoofing, and remote access. Ethical considerations are a guiding compass, reminding users that privacy and responsibility are inextricably intertwined. VPNs remain steadfast as the digital horizon expands—an embodiment of human ingenuity, technology's transformative potential, and the unwavering pursuit of a secure and private digital existence.

CHAPTER VII

Application Security

Securing web applications and APIs

In the intricate tapestry of the digital realm, where interactions and transactions unfold seamlessly across the virtual landscape, the vulnerabilities of web applications and APIs present a formidable challenge. The ubiquity of web-based services has revolutionized how we access information, conduct business, and communicate. Yet, the digital storefronts facilitating these interactions are not immune to cyber threats, data breaches, and unauthorized access. Web applications and APIs play a pivotal role in digital security as gateways between users and backend systems. This section delves into the intricate world of securing web applications and APIs, exploring the manifold threats they face, dissecting the principles of secure development, analyzing authentication and authorization mechanisms, and underscoring the ongoing commitment to vigilance and resilience in the face of evolving cyber risks.

Web applications and APIs (Application Programming Interfaces) are the conduits that connect users with digital services and data. Web applications facilitate user interactions through browsers, enabling tasks ranging from online shopping to social networking. APIs, on the other hand, allow different software systems to communicate and exchange information seamlessly. This interconnected landscape has transformed industries and user experiences, yet it has also opened doors for cyber adversaries to exploit vulnerabilities and compromise the security of these digital gateways.

Web applications and APIs present an expansive attack surface—a wide array of potential entry points for cyber attackers. Threats encompass injection attacks, such as SQL injection and cross-site scripting (XSS), which exploit vulnerabilities in code to manipulate data or execute malicious scripts. Other threats include cross-site request forgery (CSRF), where attackers control user actions, and broken authentication and session management, which could lead to unauthorized access. As the digital ecosystem evolves, so do the creative methods by which attackers seek to exploit these vulnerabilities.

The web application and API security foundation is rooted in secure development practices. Adopting safe coding principles, adherence to best practices, and regular security assessments are pivotal. Developers must sanitize input data, validate and escape output, and employ parameterized queries to thwart injection attacks. Implementing security headers, using encryption for sensitive data, and employing Content Security Policies (CSP) further fortify applications against threats.

Authentication and authorization form the bedrock of access control, determining who can access web applications and APIs and what actions they can perform. Authentication entails verifying the identity of users through credentials like usernames and passwords or more advanced methods like multi-factor authentication (MFA). Authorization, conversely, defines the actions users are authorized to perform once authenticated. Employing the principle of least privilege ensures that users have only the permissions necessary for their tasks, reducing the potential impact of a breach.

API security poses a unique challenge due to the nature of their interactions. APIs connect disparate systems and services, and any vulnerability in an API can expose a broad range of data and functionality. Implementing proper authentication mechanisms, like OAuth and API keys, is crucial. Rate limiting, which restricts the number of API requests from a single source, prevents abuse and reduces the risk of denial-of-service attacks. Secure coding practices and input validation are equally essential in the API landscape.

Open Web Application Security Project, also called OWASP, stands as a beacon in the realm of web application security. OWASP's Top Ten Project outlines the most critical security risks for web applications, offering a comprehensive guide to developers and security professionals. The project underscores the importance of vulnerability awareness, secure coding practices, and continual vigilance in identifying and mitigating emerging threats.

A holistic approach to web application and API security involves integrating security practices throughout the software development lifecycle. Security considerations must be woven into each phase from design and coding up to testing and deployment. Threat modeling, code reviews, and penetration testing identify vulnerabilities early, enabling developers to remediate issues before they reach production environments.

Third-party components and services play a pivotal role in web application and API development in the interconnected digital landscape. However, they also introduce potential risks. It is essential to assess the security practices of third-party vendors, scrutinizing their security controls, adherence to best practices, and history of security incidents. Regular audits and ongoing monitoring of third-party components mitigate the risk of vulnerabilities or breaches stemming from external sources.

The digital landscape is dynamic, and so are the threats that traverse it. Securing web applications and APIs is an ongoing commitment—an ever-evolving process that demands vigilance and resilience. Regular security assessments, continuous monitoring, and proactive threat hunting ensure that vulnerabilities are promptly identified and mitigated. As new vulnerabilities emerge, patches and updates must be swiftly deployed to maintain a robust security posture.

In conclusion, securing web applications and APIs is a testament to the harmonization of technology, human expertise, and an unwavering commitment to digital resilience. In an age where interactions, transactions, and experiences are increasingly mediated through digital interfaces, protecting these gateways is not a choice—it's a necessity. By adhering to secure development practices, fortifying authentication and authorization mechanisms, and remaining vigilant in the face of evolving threats, organizations and developers can confidently navigate the complex web of digital interactions. The guardianship of web applications and APIs is not a fleeting responsibility—it's an enduring commitment to ensuring that the digital landscape remains a realm where innovation thrives and cyber threats are met with unwavering resolve.

The role of secure coding practices

In the intricate realm of software development, where lines of code shape digital landscapes and bring ideas to life, the quest for functionality and innovation is intrinsically tied to the imperative of security. In an era marked by interconnected systems, intricate applications, and the relentless evolution of cyber threats, the role of secure coding practices stands as a sentinel—fortifying the digital fortresses against the ceaseless tide of vulnerabilities, exploits, and breaches. This section delves into the multifaceted landscape of secure coding, unraveling its principles, examining its significance in modern software development, exploring the threats it mitigates, and underscoring the collaboration between human expertise and technological innovation in shaping a more resilient digital ecosystem.

At its core, secure coding is a philosophy—a set of principles and practices prioritizing security as an integral part of the software development lifecycle. These principles are woven into the very fabric of code, shaping its architecture, functionality, and interactions. Secure coding mandates using techniques that mitigate vulnerabilities, thwart potential exploits, and minimize the attack surface. Developers embrace principles like input validation, proper error handling, secure authentication and authorization, and the principle of least privilege. These foundational elements form the bedrock upon which secure software is built.

The digital realm is a battleground—a theater where adversaries armed with sophisticated tools and tactics seek to exploit vulnerabilities in software. The threat landscape encompasses an array of attack vectors, from injection attacks like SQL injection and cross-site scripting (XSS) to authentication bypass and privilege escalation. Each vulnerability allows attackers to compromise data, breach systems, and infiltrate networks. Secure coding practices act as a bulwark against these threats, closing the door on potential exploits and ensuring that software remains resilient in the face of adversity.

While technology is an enabler, the human factor is the linchpin in secure coding practices. Armed with an understanding of the threat landscape, developers must cultivate a security mindset that instinctively questions assumptions, anticipates potential weaknesses, and strives for a holistic view of the software's security posture. Continuous learning, adherence to best practices, and a commitment to incorporating security measures into each development phase underscore the human role in crafting robust defenses.

Secure coding practices do not exist in isolation—they must coexist harmoniously with the pursuit of functionality, user experience, and innovation. Striking this balance is pivotal, as overly restrictive security measures can impede user engagement and hinder the very goals that software aims to achieve. Developers must evaluate security requirements within the context of the software's purpose, embracing measures that mitigate risks without compromising user needs.

In the interconnected web of software systems, the security of an application is often only as strong as its weakest link. A single vulnerability can cascade into a breach with far-reaching consequences. Secure coding practices acknowledge the vulnerability chain, addressing potential weaknesses at multiple levels. Regular code reviews, automated security testing, and the implementation of security controls such as input validation collectively bolster the entire chain, minimizing opportunities for exploitation.

Secure coding practices are most effective when seamlessly integrated into the software development lifecycle. Security considerations must be threaded throughout from the initial design phase to coding, testing, and deployment. Threat modeling—identifying potential vulnerabilities and their potential impacts—provides a blueprint for secure development. Code reviews and static analysis tools scrutinize code for vulnerabilities before they reach production. Integrating security checkpoints into each phase ensures that secure coding is not an afterthought but a proactive endeavor.

While frameworks and libraries expedite development, they can also introduce vulnerabilities if not utilized correctly. Secure coding extends to the selection and utilization of third-party components. Developers must stay informed about updates and patches, ensuring that frameworks and libraries are up-to-date and free of known vulnerabilities. Code reuse, while efficient, must be accompanied by an awareness of potential security risks.

Secure coding practices thrive in an environment of collaboration and knowledge sharing. Developers, security professionals, and stakeholders must collaborate to identify potential threats, share best practices, and foster a culture of security consciousness. Sharing experiences, lessons learned, and emerging threat trends empowers the collective effort to elevate secure coding practices across the software development landscape.

Secure coding practices are not a destination but a journey—a lifecycle of resilience that evolves alongside the dynamic threat landscape. Integrating security into development practices, implementing secure coding standards, and using tools like static and dynamic analysis contribute to a software's ongoing defense. The rapid pace of software evolution demands continuous learning, adaptation, and vigilance to ensure that secure coding practices remain effective.

In conclusion, the role of secure coding practices is a symphony of technology, expertise, and commitment. In a digital landscape marked by ceaseless innovation and escalating cyber threats, pursuing security is not a solitary endeavor—it's a shared responsibility reverberating across industries, disciplines, and technologies. By embracing secure coding principles, weaving security into the software development lifecycle, and fostering a culture of vigilance, the digital realm becomes a landscape where functionality and security coexist harmoniously. Secure coding practices—each line of code fortified with principles of resilience—paint a portrait of human ingenuity, technological prowess, and an unwavering commitment to ensuring that digital creations are not just functional, but also safeguarded against the relentless tide of cyber vulnerabilities.

Common vulnerabilities and how to mitigate them

In the intricate tapestry of the digital landscape, where innovation and connectivity converge, vulnerabilities lurk—potential gateways through which cyber adversaries can breach systems, compromise data, and wreak havoc. The ceaseless evolution of technology brings with it an equally relentless wave of threats—each vulnerability a chink in the digital armor. Vulnerabilities are the Achilles' heel of software, applications, and systems, from injection attacks to authentication flaws. This section ventures into the realm of common vulnerabilities, exploring their manifestations, dissecting their impact, and illuminating the strategies employed to mitigate their risk. Understanding these vulnerabilities and embracing proactive measures can fortify the digital realm against the ceaseless tide of cyber threats.

Injection attacks—where malicious code is injected into data inputs—are pernicious vulnerabilities that plague software systems. SQL injection, a notorious subtype, exploits lax input validation to manipulate database queries, potentially granting attackers unauthorized access or control over databases. Similarly, cross-site scripting (XSS) targets users, injecting malicious scripts into websites that execute within their browsers. Mitigation entails rigorous input validation, parameterized queries, and output encoding to prevent code injection. Content Security Policies (CSP) are employed to thwart XSS attacks by restricting the execution of scripts from untrusted sources.

Authentication is the digital gateway that verifies users' identities, yet broken authentication allows attackers to masquerade as legitimate users. Attackers can exploit weak passwords, flaws in session management, or stolen credentials. Multi-factor authentication (MFA), enforcing strong password policies, and utilizing secure session management mechanisms mitigate this vulnerability.

Regularly auditing and monitoring authentication logs detect anomalies and unauthorized access attempts.

Sensitive data exposure, often resulting from poor encryption practices, poses a grave risk. When data is inadequately protected, it becomes a treasure trove for attackers. Encryption is the linchpin in mitigating this threat—data at rest and data in transit must be encrypted using strong algorithms. Implementing proper key management practices and adhering to data protection regulations further fortify defenses against sensitive data exposure.

XML External Entity (XXE) attacks target applications that process XML input. By exploiting parsing vulnerabilities, attackers can inject malicious XML entities that lead to data leakage, server-side request forgery (SSRF), or denial-of-service attacks. To mitigate XXE vulnerabilities, developers must validate and sanitize XML input, turn off external entity references, and use whitelisting to restrict allowed XML elements.

Misconfigured settings—whether in databases, application servers, or cloud platforms—create open doors for attackers. Default credentials, unnecessary services, and exposed sensitive information are the hallmarks of security misconfigurations. Regular security audits, adhering to hardening guidelines, and employing continuous monitoring tools identify and rectify misconfigurations before they are exploited.

Cross-Site Request Forgery (CSRF) attacks exploit users' authenticated sessions to perform actions without their consent. Attackers can manipulate account settings or perform transactions by tricking users into performing activities they did not intend. Prevention mechanisms include using anti-CSRF tokens, validating the referer header, and employing the SameSite attribute for cookies.

Integrating third-party components—frameworks, libraries, and plugins—accelerates development but introduces risks. Using outdated components with known vulnerabilities poses a significant threat. Developers must stay informed about updates, subscribe to security advisories, and continuously assess the components they use. Automated tools can aid in identifying and remedying vulnerable components.

Lack of comprehensive logging and monitoring hinders the timely detection of attacks and security incidents. Proper logging mechanisms and real-time monitoring enable rapid detection, investigation, and response to abnormal activities. Regular log reviews and implementing intrusion detection and prevention systems further bolster an organization's resilience.

APIs, the conduits through which systems communicate, are susceptible to attacks if not adequately secured. Insufficient authentication and authorization mechanisms and poor input validation expose APIs to exploitation. Implementing robust authentication methods, authorizing users based on the principle of least privilege, and validating input data are vital in securing APIs.

Unvalidated redirects and forwards occur when an attacker manipulates URLs to redirect users to malicious sites. These vulnerabilities can be exploited for phishing attacks. Mitigation involves validating user input for redirects and using whitelisting to restrict allowed destinations.

In conclusion, the digital landscape is a minefield of vulnerabilities—a symphony of risks and opportunities where secure coding practices and proactive measures play a pivotal role in shaping the course of interactions. Organizations and developers navigate the digital realm with vigilance and resilience by understanding common vulnerabilities, embracing secure development practices, and fostering a culture of security consciousness. The collaboration of human expertise and technological innovation in mitigating vulnerabilities is an enduring testament to the commitment to safeguarding digital ecosystems. Each vulnerability mitigated, each threat thwarted, paints a portrait of a digital realm where innovation thrives and the quest for security remains unwavering.

CHAPTER VIII

Security for Small Businesses

Cybersecurity considerations for small business owners

In the digital age, where commerce, communication, and collaboration thrive in the interconnected realm, small businesses are both beneficiaries and targets. The transformative power of technology offers unprecedented opportunities for growth and innovation, yet it also casts a spotlight on the vulnerabilities that cyber threats exploit. Armed with vision and determination, small business owners navigate a landscape where data breaches, ransomware attacks, and digital espionage are no longer distant probabilities, but imminent challenges. This section explores the realm of cybersecurity considerations for small business owners, delving into the threats they face, the strategies to fortify defenses, the role of employee awareness, and the enduring commitment to resilience in the face of evolving risks.

In the sprawling landscape of cyberspace, threats are no longer confined to the physical realm. Small businesses, often perceived as softer targets, face an array of cyber adversaries—hackers, cybercriminals, and even nation-states—that seek to exploit vulnerabilities for financial gain or competitive advantage. Data breaches can lead to compromised customer information, regulatory penalties, and reputational damage. Ransomware attacks can hold critical data hostage, crippling operations and demanding ransoms for release. Phishing attempts target unsuspecting employees to gain unauthorized access or compromise sensitive data. Understanding the various threats is the first step in fortifying the digital frontier.

Cybersecurity for small businesses begins with a proactive approach—identifying vulnerabilities, implementing protective measures, and creating a fortress against potential attacks. Regular software updates and patches are crucial, as attackers often exploit known vulnerabilities. Firewalls and intrusion detection systems safeguard against unauthorized access, while robust authentication mechanisms restrict entry. Data encryption, both at rest and in transit, ensures that sensitive information remains indecipherable to prying eyes. Establishing security policies, procedures, and incident response plans lays the groundwork for a coordinated defense.

The human element is both a strength and a vulnerability in the cybersecurity equation. Small business owners must recognize that employees play a pivotal role in defense—both as potential targets and as the first line of defense. Employee awareness training educates staff about phishing attempts, social engineering tactics, and best practices for secure online behavior. Regular simulated phishing exercises help gauge the effectiveness of training efforts and reinforce the importance of vigilance.

The rise of remote work, accelerated by global events, adds a layer of complexity to small business cybersecurity. Remote employees accessing networks from various locations and devices increase the attack surface. Employing virtual private networks (VPNs) encrypts data transmissions over public networks, while secure remote desktop protocols and multi-factor authentication enhance access control. Clear remote work policies and guidelines ensure that security measures are consistently applied, irrespective of location.

Small businesses often collaborate with vendors and third-party partners, expanding their digital ecosystem. However, these collaborations introduce potential risks. Vendors may have access to sensitive/personal data or systems, making their security practices pivotal. Small business owners must vet vendors for security practices, require them to adhere to cybersecurity standards, and conduct regular audits to ensure compliance.

In a digital landscape of uncertainty, responding swiftly and effectively to cyber incidents is a cornerstone of resilience. Small business owners should create and test incident response plans that outline the essential steps to take when a breach occurs. This includes notifying affected parties, law enforcement, and regulatory authorities as necessary. Backups, stored securely and regularly tested, provide a lifeline in case of data loss due to a cyber incident.

Cybersecurity is not only a matter of best practices—it's also a legal and regulatory requirement. Depending on the industry and geographic location, small businesses may be subject to data protection laws that mandate the safeguarding of customer information. Familiarity with applicable regulations and implementing measures to comply with them is essential to avoid legal repercussions.

Cybersecurity is not a one-time endeavor—it's an ongoing commitment that demands vigilance, adaptation, and a culture of security consciousness. Small business owners must foster an environment where cybersecurity is a shared responsibility. Regular security assessments, scanning of vulnerability, and penetration testing identify weak points that need remediation. Staying informed about emerging threats, attending cybersecurity training, and engaging with the broader cybersecurity community contribute to an atmosphere of resilience.

In conclusion, the digital realm is a realm of possibility and peril—a landscape where small business growth is inseparable from cybersecurity's imperative. Small business owners confidently navigate the digital frontier by understanding the threats, adopting proactive strategies, fostering employee awareness, and embracing a culture of resilience. Each investment in cybersecurity fortifies not just digital assets, but also the business's reputation, trust, and future. The journey of cybersecurity is one of perpetual evolution, where human expertise and technological innovation converge to safeguard the aspirations of small businesses in the face of an ever- changing digital landscape.

Building a cybersecurity policy and incident response plan

In the dynamic landscape of the digital age, where innovation and connectivity intersect with cyber threats, the imperative of cybersecurity transcends industries and domains. Every organization—be it a multinational corporation or a small business—is a potential target in the virtual crosshairs of cyber adversaries seeking to exploit vulnerabilities, compromise data, and disrupt operations. In this arena of escalating risks, building a robust cybersecurity policy and an effective incident response plan is not just a choice but a strategic imperative. This section navigates the intricate realm of crafting a cybersecurity policy and an incident response plan, delving into their components, the synergy between them, the role of employee training, and the enduring commitment to digital resilience in a volatile threat landscape.

A cybersecurity policy is the foundation of an organization's digital defenses. It is a strategic document that outlines the organization's stance on cybersecurity, delineates roles and responsibilities, and sets the tone for security practices. In tandem with the policy, an incident response plan is the playbook that guides the organization's actions when a cyber incident occurs. It defines the steps to take, the chain of command, and the communication strategies to mitigate the impact of breaches, breaches, or attacks.

A comprehensive cybersecurity policy covers a spectrum of elements that collectively create a resilient security posture. It begins with defining roles and responsibilities, allocating ownership of security initiatives to specific individuals or teams. Access control, authentication, and authorization policies establish the parameters for who can access what data and systems. Secure coding practices, software updates, and encryption standards safeguard applications and data. Acceptable use policies set boundaries for using organizational resources, while guidelines for remote work and BYOD (Bring Your Own Device) establish security practices for off-premises operations. The policy also outlines the organization's approach to incident response, breach notification, and regulatory compliance.

In a digital landscape fraught with uncertainties, an incident response plan is the compass that guides an organization through the storm of cyber incidents. It defines the roles and responsibilities of the incident response team, which could include representatives from IT, legal, communication, and executive leadership. It establishes a tiered response structure, detailing the actions to take when different incidents occur. From detecting and analyzing the incident to containing and eradicating the threat, the plan provides a structured approach to minimize damage and restore normal operations swiftly.

While technology is the canvas of cybersecurity, the human factor remains a critical link in the defense chain. A cybersecurity policy and incident response plan are only effective if employees are well-informed and aware of their responsibilities. Cybersecurity training sessions educate employees about phishing attempts, social engineering tactics, password hygiene, and secure online behavior. Regularly scheduled simulated phishing exercises serve as reality checks, gauging the effectiveness of training efforts and reinforcing the importance of vigilance.

A well-crafted cybersecurity policy and an effective incident response plan are not standalone entities—they are interwoven threads that collectively shape an organization's digital resilience. The cybersecurity policy sets the groundwork for secure practices and provides the context for incident response actions. The incident response plan, on the other hand, translates policy into action, dictating the step-by-step process to address cyber incidents. The synergy between the two documents ensures that security measures are aligned with the organization's overarching goals and are seamlessly executed in the event of an incident.

In the realm of cybersecurity, uncertainty reigns supreme. Organizations cannot predict the exact nature or timing of cyber incidents, but they can prepare for them through scenario planning. By simulating various types of cyber incidents, organizations test the efficacy of their incident response plans, identify gaps, and fine-tune their strategies. Scenario planning enhances preparedness and fosters a culture of resilience where employees are equipped to handle unforeseen challenges.

The digital threat landscape is in a perpetual state of flux, demanding organizations to adapt and evolve alongside it. A cybersecurity policy and incident response plan are not static artifacts—they are living documents that must be reviewed and updated regularly. As new threats emerge and technologies evolve, the policy and plan must be amended to address the changing reality. Regular drills, tabletop exercises, and post-incident reviews provide learning, refinement, and continuous improvement opportunities.

Building a cybersecurity policy and an incident response plan requires leadership to set the tone and prioritize security across the organization. Leadership buy-in ensures policies are enforced, resources are allocated, and training initiatives receive support. A security-conscious culture starts from the top, with executives leading by example and demonstrating a commitment to digital resilience.

In conclusion, the digital landscape is a realm of both promise and peril—an arena where innovation and cyber threats coexist. Crafting a cybersecurity policy and an incident response plan is not just a compliance exercise but a strategic imperative. Organizations build a resilient foundation by creating a comprehensive policy, defining roles, and setting security standards. The incident response plan, the organization's playbook for navigating cyber storms, translates policy into action, minimizing damage and restoring normalcy. The synergy between policy, plan, and employee awareness forms the bedrock of digital resilience, ensuring that organizations can develop in the digital era while navigating the uncharted waters of cyber threats. The journey of cybersecurity is one of ongoing adaptation and vigilance, where the commitment to safeguarding digital assets is a testament to an organization's dedication to preserving its future.

Protecting customer data and maintaining trust

In the huge expanse of the digital realm, where interactions, transactions, and relationships unfold seamlessly across virtual landscapes, trust is the cornerstone of business success. For every organization, from startups to multinational corporations, preserving customer data integrity is not just a responsibility—it's a sacred duty. The interconnectedness of modern commerce brings convenience and innovation, but it also casts a spotlight on the vulnerabilities that can compromise customer trust. In this era of escalating cyber threats, safeguarding customer data and maintaining trust is not just a compliance checkbox—it's a strategic imperative. This section navigates the intricate domain of protecting customer data, examining the significance of data privacy, the challenges of cybersecurity, the role of regulatory compliance, and the enduring commitment to fostering trust in the digital age.

In the digital age, data is more than just bits and bytes—it's the currency of trust. Organizations collect, process, and store a staggering amount of customer data, from personal information to transaction histories. This treasure trove is the key to personalized experiences, informed decision-making, and improved customer engagement. However, with the privilege of data comes the responsibility to protect it from cyber threats and breaches that can erode customer trust. Data privacy is the bedrock upon which this trust is built, ensuring that customer information is treated with the highest level of care and security.

Cyber adversaries, equipped with sophisticated tools and tactics, exploit vulnerabilities to breach systems, compromise data, and undermine customer trust. Data breaches not only expose sensitive information but also lead to financial losses, legal repercussions, and reputational damage. Ransomware attacks can hold data hostage, crippling operations and demanding ransoms for release. Phishing attempts target customers' personal information, leading to identity theft and financial fraud. Understanding these threats is the first step toward constructing a digital fortress that guards customer data and trust.

As data breaches make headlines and customers become increasingly aware of privacy risks, governments and regulatory bodies have responded by enacting stringent data protection laws. Regulations like the European Union's GDPR and the CCPA in the United States empower customers by granting them control over their data. Organizations must obtain explicit consent for data collection, inform customers about data usage, and provide mechanisms for data deletion. Compliance with these regulations safeguards customers' rights and reinforces trust by demonstrating a commitment to responsible data handling.

Transparency is the cornerstone of customer trust in the digital era. Organizations must communicate openly with customers about how their data is collected, processed, and utilized. Privacy policies should be clear, concise, and easily accessible. Organizations should avoid obfuscation or hidden agendas when it comes to customer data. Communicating security measures and cybersecurity practices helps customers understand the efforts to protect their information, reinforcing trust through transparency.

Security is not an afterthought—it's a fundamental design principle. Implementing security by design ensures that customer data protection is woven into every aspect of an organization's operations. Security measures are incorporated from the ground up, from software development to data storage and transmission. Secure coding practices, encryption, access controls, and regular security assessments are integral components of this approach. A security-conscious culture empowers employees to consider data protection at every turn.

The human factor is the greatest strength and vulnerability in data protection. Whether in customer service, IT, or marketing, employees play a pivotal role in safeguarding customer data. Data privacy training educates employees about the importance of confidentiality, secure communication, and adherence to data protection protocols. Regular training sessions instill a culture of vigilance and accountability, ensuring that customer data is handled with the utmost care.

In a digital landscape fraught with uncertainties, incidents are not a question of "if" but "when." An effective incident response plan is the organization's playbook to navigate the storm of breaches. The plan outlines the steps to take, the communication strategies to employ, and the roles and responsibilities of incident response teams. A well-executed incident response mitigates damage and demonstrates an organization's commitment to customer trust by swiftly addressing breaches and keeping customers informed.

Collaboration with vendors and third-party partners extends the circle of trust beyond the organization's walls. These collaborations often involve data sharing and access to customer information. It's imperative to vet vendors for their data protection practices, ensuring they adhere to similar privacy and security standards. Contracts should outline data handling obligations and require compliance with data protection regulations.

In the aftermath of a data breach, transparency becomes an even more critical component of maintaining customer trust. Promptly notifying affected customers, being honest about the nature of the breach, and outlining the steps taken to address it are essential. Organizations should provide resources for customers to protect themselves, such as offering credit monitoring services. Organizations can begin rebuilding trust by demonstrating ownership, accountability, and a commitment to rectifying the situation.

In conclusion, the digital age is a realm of empowerment and vulnerability—a landscape where customer trust is the fulcrum upon which success pivots. Protecting customer data is not only just a legal or regulatory obligation—it's a pact of integrity that resonates with responsible business values. Organizations forge an unbreakable bond of trust with customers by embracing data privacy, adopting security by design principles, fostering transparency, and prioritizing employee training. Each safeguard, each vigilantly crafted policy, and each resilient response to breaches is a testament to an organization's dedication to preserving customer trust. The journey of data protection is one of ongoing adaptation, where the commitment to safeguarding customer data becomes the armor that fortifies the bridge between organizations and the customers they serve.

CHAPTER IX

Emerging Technologies and Threats

Exploring AI-driven cybersecurity solutions

In the ever-evolving cybersecurity landscape, where technology and threats entwine in a constant battle for supremacy, a new vanguard has emerged—a fusion of human ingenuity and machine intelligence known as AI-driven cybersecurity solutions. As the digital realm expands and becomes more intricate, cyber threats have evolved from isolated incidents to sophisticated, persistent attacks that challenge even the most robust security measures. In this complex realm of adversaries and defenders, artificial intelligence has emerged as a game-changer, promising to revolutionize how organizations detect, prevent, and respond to cyber threats. This section delves into AI-driven cybersecurity solutions, exploring their capabilities, applications, challenges, and the dynamic landscape they shape.

Artificial Intelligence, a technological marvel that simulates human intelligence, has traversed numerous domains, from language processing to image recognition. In cybersecurity, AI augments human capabilities by processing vast volumes of data, identifying patterns, and detecting anomalies that may elude human analysts. Machine learning, a subset of AI, equips systems to learn from data and enhance their performance over time. This potent combination transforms AI into a force multiplier, amplifying the effectiveness of cybersecurity measures. AI-driven cybersecurity solutions encompass a multifaceted arsenal of tools to tackle diverse threats.

Intrusion Detection Systems (IDS) fortified by AI analyze network traffic patterns, swiftly identifying anomalies and potential breaches. AI-powered threat intelligence systems scour the digital landscape for emerging threats, providing organizations with real-time insights to bolster defenses. Behavioral analytics, another AI-driven approach, scrutinizes user behavior to detect deviations from normal patterns, flagging potential insider threats. Predictive analytics, driven by AI, anticipate vulnerabilities and enable proactive patching.

The traditional approach to incident response is retrospective—a reaction to an already occurring event. AI injects a dose of anticipation by analyzing historical data, identifying trends, and predicting potential vulnerabilities. In the event of a breach, AI-driven incident response orchestrates swift and surgical actions, containing the threat, minimizing damage, and facilitating a faster recovery. The marriage of AI and human expertise transforms incident response from a reactive firefighting operation into a proactive defense strategy.

Threat hunting, a proactive approach to cybersecurity, involves actively seeking out threats that may have eluded automated defenses. AI empowers threat hunters by sifting through mountains of data, detecting subtle indicators of compromise, and uncovering hidden threats. The marriage of AI-driven analytics with human intuition empowers organizations to navigate the shadows of the digital realm with unprecedented precision.

While the promises of AI-driven cybersecurity solutions are tempting, they are not without challenges. Adversaries armed with AI-driven tools can develop strategies to bypass AI-based defenses, leading to a cat-and-mouse game of evolving tactics. The "black box" nature of some AI algorithms can hinder transparency, making it difficult to understand the rationale behind decisions. Bias in AI algorithms, if not mitigated, can lead to discriminatory or inaccurate outcomes. Additionally, the shortage of skilled AI cybersecurity professionals hinders the widespread adoption of AI-driven solutions.

The synergy between human expertise and AI intelligence is pivotal in cybersecurity. AI amplifies the capabilities of human analysts, processing vast volumes of data and identifying subtle patterns. However, human intuition, contextual understanding, and creative problem-solving remain essential in interpreting complex threats and making strategic decisions. The future of cybersecurity lies in the harmonious collaboration between AI and human defenders—a symphony of expertise that anticipates threats, thwarts attacks, and fortifies digital landscapes.

As AI assumes a more significant role in cybersecurity, ethical considerations emerge. Using AI to predict and prevent attacks raises questions about privacy and surveillance. Ensuring that AI algorithms are without bias is crucial to avoid discriminatory outcomes. Transparency in AI-driven decision-making is essential to build trust among stakeholders. Ethical guidelines and frameworks must be established to navigate the moral landscape of AI-driven cybersecurity.

The landscape of AI-driven cybersecurity is not static—it's a journey marked by continuous evolution and adaptation. Machine learning models must be trained on ever-evolving threat data to remain effective. Algorithms must be refined to reduce false positives and negatives. New threats will emerge, demanding the creation of novel AI solutions. As AI evolves, so do cyber threats, creating a perpetual cycle of innovation and response.

In conclusion, AI-driven cybersecurity solutions stand at the intersection of technology and security—a convergence that promises to reshape how organizations defend their digital territories. As AI enhances threat detection, streamlines incident response, and empowers threat hunters, it becomes an indispensable ally in the ongoing battle against cyber adversaries. The synergy between AI and human expertise heralds a new era of defense—one where anticipation trumps reaction and resilience prevails over vulnerability. However, the promises of AI are accompanied by challenges that demand ethical considerations, transparency, and continuous refinement. The journey of AI-driven cybersecurity is not a destination but an ongoing exploration of possibilities and solutions safeguarding today's and tomorrow's digital realms.

Risks and benefits of IoT devices

In the modern digital landscape, where technology is seamlessly integrated into daily life, the Internet of Things (IoT) emerges as a transformative force. IoT devices, ranging from smart thermostats to connected wearable devices, have ushered in an era of unparalleled convenience, connectivity, and innovation. However, this remarkable progress is accompanied by a dual-edged sword—a symphony of risks and benefits that define the IoT landscape. This section delves into the multifaceted world of IoT devices, exploring the potential they unlock, the vulnerabilities they expose, the privacy challenges they present, and the overarching considerations that guide their journey.

At the heart of the IoT lies the promise of enhanced efficiency, convenience, and connectivity. Smart homes adorned with IoT devices enable homeowners to control lighting, thermostats, and appliances remotely. Healthcare embraces wearable IoT devices that monitor vital signs and transmit real-time data to healthcare professionals, fostering proactive care. Smart cities leverage IoT to optimize traffic flow, conserve energy, and enhance urban living. Industrial IoT revolutionizes manufacturing and supply chains, delivering predictive maintenance and real-time monitoring. IoT sensors track soil conditions and crop health in agriculture, optimizing yields. These benefits, fueled by data-driven insights, epitomize the transformative potential of IoT.

The IoT fabric is interwoven with threads of innovation that redefine industries and propel technology forward. By creating a mesh of interconnected devices, IoT catalyzes the creation of intelligent ecosystems that communicate, share data, and make autonomous decisions. Businesses leverage IoT to gain actionable insights into customer behavior, allowing personalized services and targeted marketing. IoT-driven telemedicine transcends geographical boundaries in healthcare, delivering healthcare to remote areas. As IoT expands, the potential to revolutionize sectors from transportation to agriculture remains boundless.

The interconnectedness that IoT devices bring can inadvertently expose individuals to privacy risks. The data generated and transmitted by IoT devices—ranging from location data to personal preferences—can be collected, analyzed, and exploited. The pervasive nature of IoT can lead to surveillance concerns, as devices potentially capture intimate aspects of daily life. Inadequate data protection measures and lax security practices can result in unauthorized access, breaches of data, and the leakage of sensitive information. The difficulty lies in balancing the benefits of connectivity and the protection of individual privacy.

By virtue of their interconnectedness, IoT devices create a sprawling attack surface that cyber adversaries can exploit. Insecure default settings, lack of regular software updates, and limited processing power can render IoT devices vulnerable to attacks. Botnets, comprised of compromised IoT devices, can launch large-scale Distributed Denial of Service (DDoS) attacks, disrupting online services. Privacy-invading attacks can lead to the exposure of personal information. The convergence of IoT and critical infrastructure introduces the potential for cyber attacks that disrupt public services and compromise safety. Addressing these security challenges is imperative to mitigate risks.

As the potential risks of IoT devices become more evident, governments and regulatory bodies are taking action to ensure consumer safety and privacy. Regulations such as the GDPR and the CCPA require organizations to acquire explicit consent for data collection, inform users about data usage, and provide mechanisms for data deletion. These regulations obligate IoT device manufacturers to adhere to data protection standards and transparent practices. While regulatory response is necessary, the dynamic nature of technology demands agility in crafting policies that balance innovation and regulation.

The proliferation of IoT devices raises ethical considerations that guide their development and deployment. IoT devices must be designed with security and privacy as core principles. Data collection, usage, and sharing transparency is essential to build and maintain user trust. Manufacturers must ensure that data collection is purposeful, consent-driven, and aligned with user expectations. As IoT devices increasingly become part of daily life, the ethical responsibility to protect individual rights becomes paramount.

While the spotlight often rests on the technological aspects of IoT, the human factor remains pivotal. Users must be educated about the privacy and security implications of IoT devices. Empowering users to understand device functionalities, manage privacy settings, and update firmware helps them actively safeguard their digital lives. Cybersecurity awareness campaigns, resources, and user-friendly interfaces can bridge the gap between technological complexity and user understanding.

The journey of IoT is a testament to human innovation, curiosity, and the pursuit of progress. However, innovation must be balanced with responsibility. Organizations that develop and manufacture IoT devices must prioritize security, privacy, and transparency. Regulatory bodies must craft policies that foster innovation while safeguarding individual rights. Users must embrace IoT devices with a critical understanding of their implications. Society must engage in a dialogue about the boundaries and ethics of IoT deployment.

In conclusion, IoT devices are the threads that weave the fabric of a connected future—a landscape of possibilities and challenges. The benefits of enhanced efficiency, innovation, and convenience come hand in hand with risks to privacy, security, and ethical considerations. As the IoT landscape continues to evolve, stakeholders—manufacturers, regulators, and users—must work collaboratively to navigate the uncharted territories of connectivity. The journey of IoT is not merely a technological odyssey—it's a reflection of our values, choices, and commitment to shaping a digital landscape that empowers, enriches, and protects.

Potential impact of quantum computing on cybersecurity

In the intricate realm of technology, where innovation propels us forward into uncharted territories, quantum computing emerges as a beacon of possibility and disruption. With promises of exponential computational power, quantum computing has the potential to reshape industries and revolutionize problem-solving. However, this revolutionary force comes with an enigmatic shadow—the potential to render traditional cryptographic methods obsolete, unveiling a seismic impact on cybersecurity. This section ventures into the intricate nexus of quantum computing and cybersecurity, exploring its promises, the vulnerabilities it exposes, the quest for quantum-safe cryptography, and the strategic preparations required to navigate this digital Rubicon.

At the heart of quantum computing lies the bewildering phenomenon of quantum bits or qubits, which can exist in numerous states simultaneously due to the principles of superposition and entanglement. Harnessing these principles, quantum computers can potentially solve complex problems exponentially faster than classical computers. This quantum leap in computational power opens doors to previously insurmountable challenges, from drug discovery to optimization problems. However, the exponential advantage of quantum computing isn't confined to benefits alone—it also extends to its implications for cryptography, posing a formidable challenge to the foundations of digital security.

While quantum computing has the ability to break cryptographic codes that secure today's digital communications, it also offers a paradoxical solution—quantum cryptography. Traditional cryptographic methods, which rely on the difficulty of factoring large numbers, can be swiftly solved by a quantum computer using Shor's algorithm. This allows malicious actors to decipher sensitive information, from financial transactions to state secrets. Yet, quantum cryptography, which leverages the principles of quantum mechanics for secure communication, promises unbreakable encryption through the inherent properties of qubits. The race is on to deploy quantum-safe cryptographic methods before quantum adversaries can breach conventional encryption.

The advent of quantum computing demands a reevaluation of the threat landscape. If intercepted and stored by adversaries, confidential information transmitted today could be decrypted once quantum computers become powerful enough. The ramifications extend beyond data breaches—digital signatures, used to verify the authenticity of messages and transactions, could be forged, leading to identity theft and fraud. Public-key infrastructure, which underpins secure communications, could crumble in the face of quantum attacks. The specter of quantum adversaries creates an urgency to fortify cybersecurity measures with quantum- resistant solutions.

The pursuit of quantum-safe cryptography seeks to design encryption methods impervious to quantum attacks. Post-quantum cryptography explores new mathematical approaches that remain secure even in the existence of quantum adversaries. Lattice-based cryptography, code-based cryptography, and multivariate polynomial cryptography are some of the contenders in the quest for quantum-resilient solutions. Standardization bodies and researchers collaborate to develop quantum-safe cryptographic algorithms, ensuring that the transition to quantum-resistant encryption is seamless and timely.

The transition to quantum-safe cryptography is not just an isolated effort—it's a sweeping transformation that requires collaboration and proactive planning. Organizations, particularly those dealing with sensitive data, must assess their digital infrastructure for vulnerabilities to quantum attacks. They must embark on a migration path toward quantum-resistant encryption before quantum adversaries can exploit conventional methods. Governments, academia, and industry must collaborate to guarantee that quantum-safe cryptographic algorithms are standardized and universally adopted, fostering a secure, resilient digital landscape against quantum threats.

Strategic considerations emerge as the chess game between quantum computing and cybersecurity unfolds. Organizations must balance the urgency to adopt quantum-safe cryptography with the feasibility of integrating these new methods into existing systems. A hybrid approach may be the pragmatic solution, where classical and quantum-resistant encryption coexists. Simultaneously, research and development efforts must continue to push the boundaries of quantum-safe cryptography, staying ahead of the curve in the quantum race.

The advent of quantum computing raises ethical and policy considerations that traverse the intersection of science, security, and governance. Ethical discussions center around the responsible use of quantum computing power—how it can be harnessed for positive advancements without compromising privacy or security. Policymakers must grapple with the implications of quantum supremacy, ensuring that legislation and international agreements govern the responsible use of quantum computing in the realm of cybersecurity.

In the grand tapestry of technological evolution, the advent of quantum computing marks a distinct chapter—one laden with promises and perils. The potential to expedite scientific discoveries, optimize industries, and transform problem-solving is profound. However, the possibility of unraveling the cryptographic foundations of digital security demands a proactive response. The journey ahead is one of strategic preparation, collaboration, and innovation—a journey that bridges the quantum divide and ensures that as we unlock the mysteries of the quantum realm, we fortify the guardianship of our digital frontiers.

CHAPTER X

Government Regulations and Compliance

Overview of cybersecurity regulations (e.g., GDPR, HIPAA)

In the dynamic realm of technology, where digital landscapes expand and intertwine, safeguarding data and privacy has given rise to a web of cybersecurity regulations. These regulations, crafted by governments and governing bodies, serve as a compass to navigate the intricate maze of data protection, privacy, and cyber resilience. Prominent regulations such as the General Data Protection Regulation, also known as GDPR, and the Health Insurance Portability and Accountability Act, or HIPAA, stand as sentinels, guarding individual rights and setting standards for organizations across industries. This section embarks on a journey through the expanse of cybersecurity regulations, exploring their origins, objectives, impact, and the global push for harmonization.

The genesis of cybersecurity regulations lies in recognizing the profound effect of technology on our lives. As digital transactions, data sharing, and online interactions became ubiquitous, the need for legal frameworks to protect individuals and organizations from cyber threats emerged. Regulations were crafted to establish guidelines for data handling, breach notification, and security practices. The landmark General Data Protection Regulation (GDPR), enacted by the European

Union in 2018, became a cornerstone for data protection, setting a precedent for stringent regulations that transcend borders.

The General Data Protection Regulation (GDPR) is a testament to the growing importance of data privacy and protection in the digital age. Enforced by the European Union, GDPR grants individuals control over their personal data, mandating organizations to obtain explicit consent for data collection, use, and storage. Organizations are required to provide clear privacy policies, facilitate data access requests, and promptly report data breaches. The extraterritorial reach of GDPR affects organizations worldwide that handle EU citizens' data, compelling them to adopt stringent data protection measures.

The HIPAA takes center stage in healthcare. Enacted in the United States, HIPAA ensures the confidentiality, integrity, as well as availability of protected health information. Covered entities, like healthcare providers and insurance companies, must implement administrative, technical, as well as physical safeguards to protect patient data. The HIPAA Security Rule outlines specific requirements for electronically protected health information, ensuring that healthcare entities embrace technology without compromising patient privacy.

While GDPR and HIPAA are prominent regulations, their impact is not isolated. A global shift toward strengthening cybersecurity and data protection is evident, driven by recognizing the interconnectedness of digital ecosystems. Countries worldwide are enacting regulations that mirror the principles of GDPR and HIPAA. The California Consumer Privacy Act in the United States grants consumers control over their data, similar to GDPR. Brazil's General Data Protection Law (LGPD) follows the same trajectory, underscoring the international momentum for robust cybersecurity regulations.

For organizations, cybersecurity regulations herald a dual impact—compliance obligations and enhanced cyber resilience. The compliance landscape is marked by the need to adhere to stringent data protection practices, maintain clear communication with users, and promptly address data breaches. While compliance may be perceived as a burden, it catalyzes elevating cybersecurity practices. Organizations are compelled to implement strong security measures, conduct risk assessments, and foster a data protection culture. By aligning with regulations, organizations safeguard customer trust and enhance their ability to withstand cyber threats.

One of the pivotal aspects of cybersecurity regulations is the mandate for data breach notification. Organizations must promptly inform affected individuals and regulatory authorities in case of a breach. This paradigm shift in transparency ensures that users are informed about potential risks to their data, allowing them to take necessary precautions. Data breach notification empowers individuals and holds organizations accountable for their cybersecurity practices.

While cybersecurity regulations serve noble objectives, they also introduce challenges and complexities. Compliance can be a resource-intensive endeavor, particularly for small and medium-sized enterprises. Organizations operating in multiple jurisdictions must navigate a patchwork of regulations, leading to legal ambiguity and compliance fatigue. Striking a balance between data protection and innovation can be intricate, as stringent regulations may stifle technological advancements. Furthermore, the rapid pace of technological evolution requires regulations to remain adaptable and responsive.

As the digital world becomes more interconnected, the need for harmonization of cybersecurity regulations gains prominence. Cross-border data flows necessitate consistent standards to ensure a cohesive approach to data protection. Efforts are underway to establish international frameworks for cybersecurity and data privacy. The Budapest Convention on Cybercrime and the efforts of organizations like the International Telecommunication Union (ITU) strive to create a common ground for global cybersecurity regulations. Harmonization simplifies compliance for organizations and reinforces the global commitment to cybersecurity.

In the realm of cybersecurity regulations, education and collaboration are pivotal. Organizations must prioritize cybersecurity training for employees, empowering them to recognize threats, protect data, and adhere to compliance requirements. Collaboration between governments, businesses, and civil society fosters a holistic approach to cybersecurity, with stakeholders collectively addressing threats and sharing best practices. Ethical considerations, privacy concerns, and the socio-economic impact of regulations must be openly discussed to ensure that cybersecurity regulations align with societal values.

In the intricate realm of technology and regulation, cybersecurity regulations emerge as the lodestar that guides the digital voyage. Regulations like GDPR and HIPAA underscore the significance of data protection, privacy, and resilience. As the global landscape shifts toward harmonization, the path forward involves collaborative efforts, adaptable frameworks, and a shared commitment to cybersecurity. In this interconnected world, the evolution of cybersecurity regulations is a testament to our determination to safeguard our digital spaces, ensuring that our values and rights remain steadfastly protected as technology advances.

Navigating compliance requirements

In the ever-evolving cybersecurity landscape, where digital realms intersect with regulatory frameworks, the journey towards safeguarding sensitive data and fortifying digital landscapes is marked by the complex path of compliance requirements. Compliance serves as a compass, guiding organizations through the complex terrain of data protection, privacy regulations, and cybersecurity standards. This section embarks on an expedition into the intricacies of navigating compliance requirements in cybersecurity, unraveling the significance of compliance, the multifaceted dimensions it encompasses, the challenges it presents, and the strategies organizations deploy to navigate this intricate voyage.

Compliance is the linchpin that connects cybersecurity with legal and regulatory frameworks, intertwining the imperative of data protection with the mandates set forth by governing bodies. It ensures that organizations adhere to established standards, regulations, and best practices, fostering a culture of cybersecurity that prioritizes data integrity, confidentiality, and availability. Compliance requirements act as a safeguard, shielding both organizations and individuals from the pervasive threat landscape that seeks to exploit vulnerabilities.

The cybersecurity compliance canvas is painted with a rich tapestry of regulations, standards, and directives that vary across industries and jurisdictions. Prominent regulations such as the GDPR and the HIPAA establish data protection and privacy benchmarks. Industry-specific standards such as Payment Card Industry Data Security Standard (PCI DSS) and the National Institute of Standards and Technology (NIST) Cybersecurity Framework outline sector-specific requirements. The complexity arises from the dynamic interplay of these regulations, each requiring tailored strategies for compliance.

Navigating compliance requires a strategic approach that aligns with organizational objectives and industry nuances. Organizations often adopt recognized frameworks that serve as compasses in their compliance journey. The NIST Cybersecurity Framework, for instance, provides a comprehensive structure for assessing and improving cybersecurity posture. ISO/IEC 27001 offers a blueprint for establishing an Information Security Management System (ISMS). These frameworks guide compliance efforts and facilitate risk assessment, mitigation, and the creation of a resilient cybersecurity infrastructure.

While compliance is essential for data protection, it can sometimes be perceived as an impediment to innovation. Organizations must strike a delicate balance between adhering to compliance requirements and driving technological advancement. Integrating new technologies, including cloud computing and IoT devices, adds complexity to compliance efforts. Forward-thinking organizations leverage compliance as an opportunity to innovate securely, adopting emerging technologies while ensuring that they align with regulatory standards.

The journey through compliance waters is not without challenges. The evolving nature of cybersecurity threats necessitates dynamic responses, rendering compliance an ongoing effort. The intricacies of data classification, retention, and handling require meticulous attention to detail. Global operations demand an understanding of cross-border data flow regulations. Small and medium-sized enterprises (SMEs) face resource constraints, making compliance resource-intensive. The specter of non-compliance looms large, carrying legal, financial, and reputational repercussions.

The success of navigating compliance requirements hinges on the human element—employees who embody the organization's cybersecurity culture. Training and awareness programs are crucial to equip employees with the knowledge to recognize threats, adhere to security protocols, and safeguard sensitive data. A culture of compliance extends beyond policies—it becomes a shared responsibility woven into the fabric of daily operations.

The journey through compliance is not solitary—it's an ecosystem that thrives on collaboration. Governments, regulatory bodies, industries, and organizations must collaborate to foster a robust compliance framework. International collaborations, such as the Cybersecurity Tech Accord, create a united front against cyber threats. Regulatory bodies must be adaptive, crafting relevant regulations amidst technological evolution. Regardless of size, organizations must view compliance as a shared responsibility contributing to the collective defense against cyber adversaries.

Organizations deploy a myriad of strategies to navigate compliance requirements. Risk assessment is a cornerstone—identifying vulnerabilities, evaluating their impact, and devising mitigation strategies. Regular audits assess compliance status, identify gaps, and drive remediation efforts. Automation streamlines compliance by tracking changes, generating reports, and alerting stakeholders to anomalies. Continuous monitoring ensures compliance is not a static achievement but a dynamic pursuit.

As technology advances, compliance requirements evolve. Emerging technologies like artificial intelligence as well as quantum computing introduce new complexities that demand responsive regulations. The harmonization of global standards is a crucial endeavor, particularly in the context of cross-border data flows. The future holds the promise of more sophisticated tools for compliance management, simplifying the process and enhancing accuracy.

In the intricate realm between cybersecurity and compliance, organizations navigate through the currents of complexity, challenge, and opportunity. Compliance requirements, while multifaceted, serve as the rudder that steers the ship toward safe harbors in the digital seas. As cyber threats persist and regulations evolve, the art of navigating compliance is a dynamic endeavor that requires agility, collaboration, and a commitment to securing the digital landscapes we inhabit. Just as mariners chart courses through uncharted waters, organizations chart a path through the evolving compliance landscape—a journey that leads to regulatory compliance and the fortification of trust, resilience, and a safer digital future.

Consequences of non-compliance

In the intricate tapestry of our digital age, where data flows seamlessly and technology thrives, the imperative to protect sensitive information has birthed a web of cybersecurity regulations. These regulations serve as guardians, standing sentinel over data integrity, privacy, and the resilience of digital landscapes. However, as organizations navigate this complexity of compliance, the specter of non-compliance looms ominously—a gateway to a realm of consequences that can unravel reputations, cripple operations, and erode trust. This section embarks on a voyage through the risky waters of non-compliance in cybersecurity, revealing the depths of its impact, the legal ramifications it entails, the erosion of stakeholder trust, and the strategies for avoiding this dangerous precipice.

Non-compliance in cybersecurity signifies failing to adhere to established regulations, standards, and best practices to safeguard digital assets. It exposes organizations to vulnerabilities that malicious actors can exploit, risking the confidentiality, integrity, and availability of sensitive data. Non-compliance isn't a mere procedural oversight—it's a chink in the armor that can invite cyber adversaries to breach digital fortresses, leaving a trail of devastation in their wake.

Legal ramifications form a significant aspect of the consequences of non-compliance. Regulatory bodies and governing authorities, armed with the power to impose fines and penalties, can hold organizations accountable for their negligence. The General Data Protection Regulation of European Union wields a formidable stick, with fines reaching up to 4% of global yearly turnover or €20 million, whichever is higher. Similarly, the California Consumer Privacy Act (CCPA) empowers consumers to file lawsuits against organizations for data breaches resulting from non-compliance. Due to this legal complexity, organizations may encounter financial hardship, harm to their reputation, and operational compromise.

Trust is the cornerstone of digital interactions, and non-compliance erodes this foundation. Breaches resulting from non-compliance can expose customer data, leading to identity theft, fraud, and privacy violations. The erosion of trust extends beyond immediate financial losses—it manifests as reputational damage that reverberates through both the digital and physical realms. Stakeholders, ranging from customers to partners, question an organization's commitment to their security, fostering a sense of betrayal that can have long-lasting consequences.

Non-compliance takes a heavy financial toll on organizations. Fines, penalties, and legal fees are direct costs that can drain financial resources. However, indirect costs also mount—the expenses of investigating breaches, conducting forensic analysis, and recovering from the aftermath can escalate quickly. Additionally, the erosion of stakeholder trust can lead to revenue losses as customers seek out more secure alternatives. The financial implications of non-compliance create a vicious cycle that strains resources and hampers growth.

Cybersecurity incidents resulting from non-compliance can disrupt operations in profound ways. Data breaches lead to downtime as organizations scramble to contain the breach, assess the damage, and restore systems. Regulatory investigations and legal proceedings divert resources from core operations, hampering productivity and innovation. The ripple effect extends to employees burdened with intensified workloads and uncertainty. The operational disruption caused by non-compliance jeopardizes an organization's ability to deliver products and services, further exacerbating financial losses.

In the digital age, reputation is a precious commodity. Non-compliance fractures this intangible asset, leaving organizations vulnerable to public scrutiny, media coverage, and social backlash. News of data breaches resulting from non-compliance spreads rapidly, tarnishing an organization's image and weakening its standing in the eyes of customers, partners, and investors. The painstaking effort required to rebuild a tarnished reputation can be monumental, demanding time, resources, and a strategic approach to regain lost trust.

The journey to regain the trust lost due to non-compliance is a Herculean task. Organizations must invest in transparency, accountability, and robust cybersecurity practices to demonstrate their commitment to protecting sensitive data. Swift and transparent communication in the aftermath of a breach is paramount, reassuring stakeholders that the organization takes the breach seriously and is taking concrete steps to prevent future incidents. Regaining trust involves not just rectifying past mistakes, but also fostering a culture of compliance and cybersecurity that permeates every facet of an organization.

Avoiding the consequences of non-compliance demands a proactive approach that integrates cybersecurity into every layer of an organization's operations. Organizations should implement a comprehensive cybersecurity technique that includes risk assessments, continuous monitoring, and regular audits. Compliance frameworks, such as National Institute of Standards and Technology (NIST) Cybersecurity Framework, offer a structured approach to assessing and enhancing cybersecurity posture. Regular training and awareness programs equip employees with the knowledge to identify threats and adhere to security protocols. Collaboration with regulatory bodies and industry peers fosters a collective defense against cyber threats.

The complexities of compliance necessitate a collaborative ecosystem that spans regulatory bodies, industry associations, and organizations. Regulatory bodies must provide clear guidelines and support for organizations striving to comply with evolving regulations. Industry associations facilitate the exchange of best practices and insights, allowing organizations to learn from one another's experiences. Collaboration within the ecosystem fortifies an organization's cybersecurity posture and contributes to the digital landscape's collective resilience.

In the arena of cybersecurity, non-compliance is a precipice that organizations must navigate with vigilance and dedication. The consequences of non-compliance ripple beyond financial losses—they erode trust, damage reputation, and disrupt operations. As technology develops and cyber threats become more sophisticated, the imperative to comply with regulations and standards grows more pronounced. The journey to cybersecurity excellence is a collective endeavor that requires commitment from leaders, employees, and stakeholders. As organizations traverse the stormy seas of the digital realm, the beacon of compliance serves as a guiding light —a reminder that the fortification of data, privacy, and trust remains a noble pursuit that safeguards the digital future.

CHAPTER XI

Building a Cybersecurity Mindset

Fostering a culture of cybersecurity awareness

In the interconnected landscape of the digital age, where data traverses the ethereal realm of the internet, the concept of security transcends physical boundaries. Cybersecurity, the sentinel guarding the gates of our digital fortresses, has taken center stage. Yet, in this evolving arena, the human element remains both the weakest link and the most significant asset. Fostering a culture of cybersecurity awareness is the clarion call that resonates across industries and organizations, urging individuals to become vigilant guardians of their digital lives. This section embarks on a journey through the nuances of cultivating cybersecurity awareness, exploring its significance, the challenges it encounters, strategies for effective implementation, and the role of leadership in this critical endeavor.

In a world where individuals are perpetually connected, the borders between the physical and digital realms blur. Digital footprints weave intricate tales of our lives, from financial transactions to personal communications. This heightened connectivity underscores the need for cybersecurity awareness—a state of mind where individuals recognize the potential threats that lurk in the digital shadows. Cybersecurity awareness is no longer a niche requirement; it is a fundamental skill that empowers individuals to navigate the digital landscape with prudence and resilience.

Cybersecurity awareness is the armor of individuals in the digital arena, a shield against the ceaseless barrage of cyber threats. It empowers individuals to recognize phishing emails, secure passwords, and identify malicious websites. Beyond personal safety, cybersecurity awareness extends to the workplace, safeguarding sensitive corporate data, intellectual property, and customer trust. Cybersecurity awareness serves as the first line of defense in an era where breaches can lead to financial losses, reputational damage, and legal repercussions.

Despite the advent of sophisticated technology, humans remain the fulcrum upon which cybersecurity pivots. The human element is paradoxical—it is both the weakest link and the greatest asset. Malicious actors exploit human psychology, utilizing social engineering to manipulate individuals into divulging sensitive information. Yet, when equipped with cybersecurity awareness, individuals become a formidable force. Educated employees can thwart phishing attempts, report suspicious activities, and implement security best practices that fortify the digital infrastructure.

The journey towards fostering a culture of cybersecurity awareness is challenging. The fast-paced nature of technological evolution requires constant adaptation. Training and awareness programs must stay current, addressing new threats and emerging trends. Balancing usability with security is another challenge—overly complex security measures may lead individuals to circumvent protocols, inadvertently exposing vulnerabilities. Additionally, the diversity of digital landscapes demands tailored approaches, as cybersecurity awareness in a corporate setting differs from that in a household.

Creating a culture of cybersecurity awareness necessitates a multifaceted approach. Education forms the cornerstone—comprehensive training programs familiarize individuals with the intricacies of cyber threats, instilling a sense of responsibility for their digital actions. Simulations and mock exercises expose employees to real-world scenarios, enabling them to apply their knowledge in a risk-free environment. Collaboration between IT departments and non-technical teams fosters a holistic understanding of cybersecurity. Gamification, with rewards for adhering to security protocols, injects an element of engagement into the awareness process.

The influence of leadership in cultivating cybersecurity awareness cannot be overstated. Leaders set the tone for the organization's cybersecurity culture through their actions, decisions, and communication. When leaders prioritize cybersecurity and actively participate in awareness initiatives, employees are more likely to embrace security best practices. Clear communication channels, where leaders share insights about emerging threats and the importance of cybersecurity, reinforce the significance of cybersecurity awareness across all levels of the organization.

Cultivating a culture of cybersecurity awareness is a journey towards building a resilient digital ecosystem. Employees who are well-versed in cybersecurity are assets—they can recognize threats, minimize risks, and contribute to incident response efforts. Organizations prioritizing cybersecurity awareness gain a competitive edge by enhancing customer trust, safeguarding proprietary information, and minimizing the impact of breaches. The benefits extend beyond the organization itself—when individuals practice cybersecurity awareness in their personal lives, they contribute to the overall cyber hygiene of the digital society.

The diversity of roles, responsibilities, and digital interactions demands tailored approaches to fostering cybersecurity awareness. Awareness involves staying abreast of the latest threats and vulnerabilities for technical teams. Non-technical staff may require training in recognizing social engineering tactics. Executives need insights into the business impact of cybersecurity breaches. Customized training programs that respond to the unique needs of different roles ensure that cybersecurity awareness resonates with every individual, regardless of their technical acumen.

The journey of fostering cybersecurity awareness is not a sprint—it's a marathon that requires commitment, adaptability, and a long-term vision. Awareness initiatives must be ongoing, reflecting the evolving threat landscape and technological advancements. Integrating cybersecurity awareness into organizational policies, practices, and orientations institutionalizes a culture of vigilance. Collaboration with cybersecurity experts, participation in cybersecurity events, and staying connected with industry developments keep awareness efforts relevant and effective.

As society surges forward into the digital future, the need for cybersecurity awareness illuminates the pathway. It transforms individuals from passive users into active sentinels, poised to defend against cyber threats. Just as the collective effort of individuals contributes to a resilient digital landscape, so does the sum of cybersecurity awareness efforts contribute to a safer, more secure digital society. Fostering a culture of cybersecurity awareness is not just a responsibility—it's a commitment to safeguarding our digital present and future, and a pledge to navigate the digital realm with the prudence and resilience it demands.

Continuous learning and staying updated on threats

In the ever-shifting landscape of the digital realm, where technology evolves at an unprecedented pace, the adage "knowledge is power" takes on new significance. In the realm of cybersecurity, the quest for knowledge is not a static endeavor—it's a dynamic journey of continuous learning and staying updated on evolving cyber threats. As digital ecosystems expand and cyber adversaries become more sophisticated, the imperative to remain informed becomes a cornerstone of cybersecurity resilience. This section explores the vital importance of continuous learning in the cybersecurity domain, delving into its role in cyber defense, the challenges it encounters, strategies for effective implementation, and the symbiotic relationship between human intelligence and technology.

Cybersecurity is a battlefield where malicious actors relentlessly devise new tactics to breach defenses, compromise data, and disrupt operations. Cyber threats that is ranging from ransomware attacks to social engineering schemes, mutate and adapt to circumvent security measures. As technology advances, the arsenal of threats grows, encompassing traditional cyberattacks and emerging threats like AI-driven attacks and quantum hacking. This dynamic landscape underscores the need for perpetual vigilance and an unwavering commitment to staying informed.

Continuous learning in the realm of cybersecurity is not a mere option—it's a survival imperative. Staying updated on emerging threats, vulnerabilities, and defensive strategies is the bedrock upon which effective cyber defense rests. With the proliferation of cloud computing, IoT devices, and interconnected networks, the attack surface expands, creating new avenues for cyber intrusions. Continuous learning equips cybersecurity professionals with the tools to anticipate, detect, and respond to evolving threats.

In the age of artificial intelligence and automation, the human element remains the linchpin of effective cyber defense. The ability to decipher context, recognize anomalies, and make informed decisions is a uniquely human trait that technology has yet to replicate fully. Continuous learning harnesses human intelligence, arming professionals with the knowledge to analyze complex threat vectors, assess risks, and devise adaptive countermeasures. This fusion of human understanding and technological prowess forms the foundation of resilient cybersecurity strategies.

While the digital revolution brings unprecedented opportunities, it also poses challenges in the realm of continuous learning. The quick pace of technological evolution means that cyber threats evolve quickly, rendering existing knowledge obsolete. Staying updated requires cybersecurity professionals to navigate a torrent of information—new vulnerabilities, attack techniques, and defensive strategies—that can be overwhelming. The challenge lies not only in accessing this information but also in discerning its relevance and credibility.

Staying updated on cyber threats requires a strategic approach that blends formal education, self-directed learning, and collaborative initiatives. Formal education, such as cybersecurity courses and certifications, provides a structured foundation of knowledge. Self-directed learning involves seeking information through trusted sources, online communities, and industry publications. Collaborative initiatives, such as threat intelligence sharing and participation in cybersecurity forums, leverage the community's collective expertise to disseminate up-to-date information.

Technology is both an enabler and a solution to the challenges of staying updated on cyber threats. Threat intelligence platforms aggregate real-time information about emerging threats, providing actionable insights that inform defense strategies. Automation tools analyze vast amounts of data, highlighting patterns and anomalies that human professionals might overlook. By harnessing technology, cybersecurity professionals can augment their continuous learning efforts, enabling them to focus on higher-level analysis and decision-making.

The multidimensional nature of cyber threats demands a cross-disciplinary approach to continuous learning. Cybersecurity professionals must broaden their understanding beyond traditional domains, incorporating knowledge from fields such as psychology, law, and business. Understanding the psychology behind social engineering attacks, the legal implications of data breaches, and the business impact of cyber incidents enriches the holistic comprehension of cyber threats. Cross-disciplinary learning enhances the ability to devise comprehensive defense strategies.

Leadership is pivotal in cultivating a culture of continuous learning within organizations. When leaders prioritize and invest in ongoing education, it sets a precedent that resonates throughout the workforce. Encouraging employees to pursue certifications, attend conferences, and participate in threat-sharing initiatives fosters a sense of ownership over staying informed. Leadership's commitment reinforces the understanding that continuous learning is not a solitary endeavor—it's a collective responsibility that enriches the entire organization's cybersecurity posture.

The future of continuous learning in cybersecurity lies in dynamic adaptation. Cybersecurity professionals must embrace a mindset of perpetual evolution, recognizing that the learning journey is ongoing and responsive to emerging threats. Machine learning and AI-driven analytics will further refine threat detection and prediction, enabling professionals to focus their expertise on strategic decision-making. Online education platforms, augmented reality, and virtual simulations offer innovative avenues for immersive learning experiences that simulate real-world cyber scenarios.

In the boundless expanse of cyberspace, where threats lurk in the shadows and data traverses unseen pathways, the beacon of continuous learning illuminates the path ahead. It transforms cybersecurity professionals from passive recipients of knowledge into active sentinels of digital landscapes. Just as the digital realm evolves, so must the knowledge and strategies that safeguard it. Continuous learning in cybersecurity is not just about amassing information—it's about the pursuit of resilience, the embrace of adaptation, and the commitment to securing the digital future. As technology advances and threats grow in complexity, the quest for knowledge becomes not just a choice, but a mandate—one that ensures that the defenders of cyberspace remain poised to outwit, outmaneuver, and ultimately triumph over the adversaries that seek to exploit its vulnerabilities.

Encouraging responsible online behavior

In the interconnected tapestry of the digital age, where virtual realms intertwine with daily life, responsible online behavior has emerged as an imperative that transcends boundaries. The screens that connect us also bear witness to a myriad of digital footprints, embodying our interactions, choices, and identities. As society becomes increasingly entwined with the digital landscape, the need to foster responsible online behavior takes on renewed significance. This section explores the vital role of encouraging responsible online behavior, delving into its importance, the challenges it confronts, strategies for effective implementation, and the symbiotic relationship between individual empowerment and collective digital harmony.

In an era where screens mediate human interactions, and virtual connections span the globe, responsible online behavior is an ethical compass that guides individuals through the complexity of cyberspace. From social media platforms to online financial transactions, the choices made in the digital realm hold real-world consequences. Responsible online behavior transcends demographics—a shared obligation that spans generations, professions, and cultures.

Responsible online behavior encapsulates a spectrum of actions prioritizing ethical conduct, privacy, security, and respect in the digital sphere. It encompasses a conscientious approach to sharing information, engaging in civil discourse, and curbing cyberbullying. It involves safeguarding sensitive data, adhering to copyright laws, and refraining from malicious activities compromising digital ecosystems. Responsible behavior extends to disseminating accurate information, practicing critical thinking, and fostering a vibrant, safe, and inclusive online environment.

The digital realm is a tapestry that weaves together fragments of individual identities, forming a mosaic that can influence reputations, relationships, and opportunities. Digital footprints, comprising social media posts, comments, and online interactions, create a digital dossier that is accessible to employers, colleagues, and even potential adversaries. Irresponsible behavior, such as offensive comments or sharing misleading information, can mar these digital footprints, impacting personal and professional trajectories.

Encouraging responsible online behavior isn't solely the responsibility of individuals—it's a collective endeavor that involves families, educators, policymakers, and digital platforms. Families play a pivotal role by instilling empathy, integrity, and critical thinking values in the digital realm. Educators integrate digital literacy into curricula, equipping students with the skills to explore the digital landscape responsibly. Policymakers craft regulations that curb online harassment, protect privacy, and foster digital well-being. Digital platforms implement content moderation policies, curb hate speech, and provide tools for reporting abusive behavior.

The journey to fostering responsible online behavior is marked by challenges that mirror the complexity of the digital world. The anonymity afforded by online interactions can encourage individuals to engage in harmful behavior they might not engage in face-to-face. The speed and scale of digital interactions make it challenging to track and mitigate online harassment or misinformation. Additionally, the line between freedom of expression and responsible conduct can be nebulous, necessitating nuanced approaches to regulation.

Effective strategies for encouraging responsible online behavior revolve around education, awareness, and engagement. Digital literacy programs teach individuals to recognize misinformation, identify phishing attempts, and practice secure online habits. Awareness campaigns shed light on the impact of online bullying, hate speech, and digital addiction. Engaging discussions on responsible conduct, hosted by schools, community centers, and online platforms, create spaces for dialogue and reflection.

Digital etiquette, also known as "netiquette," is integral to responsible online behavior. It encompasses the conventions and codes of conduct that govern online interactions, mirroring the etiquette of face-to-face conversations. Responding to emails promptly, refraining from using all-caps (interpreted as shouting), and avoiding excessive emojis are examples of digital etiquette. Netiquette fosters respectful communication, curbing the proliferation of negativity and fostering a culture of civility.

Leaders, whether in the corporate world, education, or government, have a profound impact on shaping responsible online behavior. By exemplifying ethical conduct in their digital interactions, leaders set a precedent that reverberates throughout their spheres of influence. In the corporate realm, leaders foster responsible behavior by crafting and enforcing policies that curb cyberbullying, safeguard data, and promote respectful communication. Educational leaders guide students in understanding the implications of their digital actions and the importance of treating digital spaces with the same respect as physical spaces.

Empowering individuals to embrace responsible online behavior requires more than rules—it demands digital literacy. Digital literacy equips individuals with the skills to evaluate online information critically, discern credible sources, and differentiate between facts and falsehoods. Digital literacy empowers individuals to make informed decisions, question narratives, and become discerning participants in the digital discourse. By arming individuals with the ability to decipher the complexities of the digital realm, digital literacy fosters a climate of responsibility.

As technology advances and digital interactions become more immersive, the landscape of digital responsibility will evolve. Artificial intelligence may play a role in content moderation and identifying online harassment. Virtual reality platforms may create spaces for empathetic conversations and simulations that foster responsible behavior. The future promises more innovative ways to cultivate digital responsibility, integrating technology into educational curricula, community initiatives, and online platforms.

In the boundless expanse of the digital cosmos, where virtual highways converge and diverge, the compass of responsible online behavior guides individuals with intention. It transforms digital denizens from passive observers into active stewards of digital harmony. Responsible online behavior isn't just about adhering to rules—it's about embodying values of empathy, integrity, and respect in a realm where the boundaries between digital and physical interactions blur. Encouraging responsible online behavior is an investment in a future where digital interactions reflect the best of human potential, where the exchange of ideas is constructive, and where digital landscapes flourish as vibrant, safe, and inclusive domains. As technology evolves and digital interactions become more integral to the human experience, the call to encourage responsible online behavior resounds as a timeless imperative that transcends pixels and screens to shape the essence of human connections in the digital age.

CHAPTER XII

The Future of Cybersecurity

Predictions for the future of cybersecurity

As the digital landscape continues to evolve exponentially, the realm of cybersecurity stands at the crossroads of innovation and challenge. In an era where technology penetrates every facet of human life, from communication to commerce, the stakes of safeguarding digital assets have never been higher. The future of cybersecurity is a tapestry woven with threads of artificial intelligence, quantum computing, shifting threat landscapes, and complex regulatory landscapes. This section explores the predictions for the future of cybersecurity, examining the emerging trends, the potential challenges, the transformative role of technology, and the strategic imperatives that will shape the cybersecurity landscape of tomorrow.

As the contours of cyberspace shift, cybersecurity trends are evolving to meet new challenges. While data protection remains paramount, the focus is expanding beyond defense to encompass digital resilience. Organizations are moving from a reactive stance to a proactive approach, integrating threat detection, incident response, and recovery into a comprehensive strategy. A shift towards more adaptable frameworks is underway, with cybersecurity becoming not just a function but an integral part of business operations.

The threat landscape is characterized by perpetual innovation—between malicious actors and cybersecurity defenders. Threats have diversified, encompassing traditional malware and emerging threats like AI-driven attacks and deepfake technology. As technology evolves, so do the attack vectors. The advent of quantum computing presents both a promise and a peril, as quantum-powered encryption could disrupt conventional security measures, leading to the development of quantum-resistant cryptography.

Machine learning and Artificial intelligence are balanced to redefine the cybersecurity paradigm. While AI and ML can be potent tools for threat detection, anomaly identification, and even autonomous incident response, they also have the potential to be exploited by malicious actors. The cat-and-mouse game between AI-driven attackers and defenders will be a defining narrative of the future. AI-powered tools can analyze massive data sets, discern patterns, and predict potential breaches, enhancing the proactive stance against cyber threats.

Quantum computing, often hailed as the harbinger of technological revolution, possesses the potential to disrupt cryptography—the very foundation of cybersecurity. Quantum computers can break existing encryption algorithms, exposing sensitive data to vulnerabilities. The emergence of quantum-resistant cryptography is a preemptive effort to address this challenge. The race is on to develop encryption methods that can withstand the computational prowess of quantum computers, safeguarding data integrity in a quantum-powered world.

In an interconnected world, regulatory landscapes are expanding to address data privacy, breach notification, and cybersecurity standards. Regulations like the General Data Protection Regulation as well as the California Consumer Privacy Act set a precedent for data protection and user rights. As organizations operate globally, compliance with diverse regulations becomes intricate.

Striking a balance between innovation and adherence to regulatory frameworks will be a pivotal challenge.

The supply chain is a vulnerable link in the cybersecurity chain, as malicious actors target third-party vendors to gain access to more extensive networks. The SolarWinds incident serves as a stark reminder of the consequences of inadequate supply chain security. Organizations are increasingly focusing on assessing the security posture of vendors and partners, emphasizing due diligence, and fostering a shared responsibility for supply chain integrity.

Amid the technological advancements, human-centric security remains pivotal. Cyber hygiene practices, such as robust password management, two-factor authentication, and recognizing phishing attempts, remain the first line of defense. Educating individuals to become vigilant stewards of their digital identities is critical to future cybersecurity strategies. The symbiotic relationship between human intelligence and technological innovation remains an enduring theme.

The requirement for skilled cybersecurity professionals continues to outpace supply, creating a workforce gap that jeopardizes the effectiveness of cybersecurity efforts. Addressing this gap requires multidimensional strategies—educational institutions must offer relevant curricula, organizations should invest in upskilling and reskilling programs, and industry collaboration should facilitate knowledge exchange. The future hinges on cultivating a diverse and adept workforce capable of adapting to the evolving threat landscape.

Geopolitical tensions spill into cyberspace, leading to the emergence of cyber warfare and diplomatic negotiations around cybersecurity norms. The world witnesses a new arena of conflict where nations deploy digital weaponry to undermine adversaries. Establishing international agreements and norms is imperative to prevent escalations in cyber conflicts. Cyber diplomacy will play a pivotal role in shaping the global cybersecurity landscape.

As the digital frontier stretches into uncharted territories, the future of cybersecurity remains a realm of both promise and uncertainty. The convergence of AI, quantum computing, and evolving threats will redefine cybersecurity. Striking a balance between innovation, compliance, and ethical considerations will be pivotal. The safeguarding of digital identities, the fortification of data resilience, and the cultivation of a human-centric security culture stand as pillars of the future. Cybersecurity professionals, policymakers, and individuals alike are poised to shape this future—a future where the digital domain is navigated with vigilance, intelligence, and a collective commitment to securing the digital landscape for future generations.

Ethical considerations in cybersecurity research and practices

In the ever-evolving realm of cybersecurity, where innovation intersects with responsibility, the ethical dimension takes center stage. As digital landscapes expand and technology becomes integral to every facet of life, the guardians of cybersecurity are entrusted with safeguarding data and upholding the values of integrity, transparency, and respect for human rights. This section embarks on a profound exploration of the ethical considerations that underpin cybersecurity research and practices, delving into their significance, the challenges they encounter, strategies for ethical decision-making, and the symbiotic relationship between technological advancement and ethical vigilance.

Ethical considerations in cybersecurity are not peripheral concerns; they form the bedrock upon which the edifice of cybersecurity stands. As technology advances, ethical considerations become pivotal in shaping cybersecurity measures' deployment, impact, and consequences. Ensuring that cybersecurity practices align with ethical standards is essential to prevent the erosion of privacy, the misuse of technology, and the exploitation of vulnerabilities. Ethical considerations extend beyond technical proficiency; they encompass values that transcend codes of conduct to safeguard the very essence of digital society.

The tension between security imperatives and individual privacy is a quintessential ethical dilemma in cybersecurity. Striking the balance between safeguarding digital assets and respecting personal privacy is a challenge that demands nuanced solutions. While robust security measures are essential, they should not infringe upon civil liberties. Ethical cybersecurity practices ensure that surveillance is targeted, proportionate, and also respectful of the rights of individuals.

Transparency is an ethical cornerstone in cybersecurity practices, especially regarding data collection, processing, and sharing. Users have the right to be informed about how their data is being used and to provide informed consent. The Facebook-Cambridge Analytica scandal is a stark reminder of the consequences of opaque data practices. Ethical cybersecurity practices prioritize transparency, clear communication, and mechanisms for individuals to exercise control over their data.

Cybersecurity tools and research can have dual uses—they can be deployed for defensive and offensive purposes. This dual-use dilemma poses ethical questions about the responsibility of cybersecurity professionals and researchers. Innovations intended to fortify security can inadvertently be weaponized by malicious actors. Ethical cybersecurity research demands careful consideration of the potential consequences of the developed tools and the contexts in which they might be employed.

The discovery of software vulnerabilities raises ethical questions about disclosure. While researchers may find vulnerabilities that malicious actors could exploit, responsible disclosure involves notifying the affected parties in a way that allows them to patch the vulnerability before it will be publicly disclosed. The timeline and method of disclosure must balance the urgency of protecting users with giving organizations sufficient time to remediate the issue.

In the interconnected digital landscape, ethical considerations transcend borders. Cybersecurity practices that operate in one jurisdiction can have implications that extend globally. This dynamic requires a cohesive approach to ethical standards that respects cultural diversity while upholding universal values. The transnational nature of cyber threats calls for international collaboration in shaping ethical norms and regulatory frameworks.

Ethical decision-making in cybersecurity is a multifaceted process that involves a blend of ethical principles, legal obligations, and stakeholder interests. Ethical frameworks like utilitarianism, deontology, and virtue ethics offer perspectives for evaluating decisions. Ethical committees, comprising cybersecurity experts, ethicists, and legal professionals, can guide in navigating complex ethical challenges. Open discussions, multidisciplinary collaboration, and ethical training cultivate a culture of ethical mindfulness.

Ethical cybersecurity practices begin with education. Incorporating ethics into cybersecurity curricula equips professionals with the tools to navigate ethical challenges. Cybersecurity programs should emphasize technical prowess and the social, legal, and ethical implications of their actions. Integrating case studies, ethical simulations, and discussions into educational settings fosters a deep understanding of ethical considerations.

Leaders in the cybersecurity domain play a pivotal role in shaping ethical practices. When leaders prioritize ethical considerations and model integrity, it sets a precedent that resonates throughout the organization. Ethical leadership involves transparent communication, creating a safe environment for raising ethical concerns, and embedding ethical considerations into organizational policies and practices.

The future of cybersecurity presents new ethical challenges as AI and automation become integral to defense strategies. The potential for autonomous decision-making raises questions about accountability and the potential for biases to be embedded in algorithms. Ethical considerations will play a vital role in shaping the ethical boundaries of AI-driven cybersecurity tools.

In a digital era where every line of code carries the weight of ethical implications, the guardians of cybersecurity are tasked with shielding data and upholding the digital world's moral compass. Ethical considerations guide the trajectory of innovation, temper the ambitions of technology, and safeguard the values that underpin human dignity. The future of cybersecurity hinges on a marriage of technical prowess with ethical mindfulness—a union that envisions a world where technological advancement is accompanied by ethical integrity, where data protection is synonymous with respect for human rights, and where the defenders of cyberspace stand as stewards of integrity, transparency, and the pursuit of a digital realm that reflects the highest aspirations of humanity.

Encouraging innovation while prioritizing security

In the boundless expanse of the digital age, where innovation is the beacon guiding progress, the realm of cyberspace stands as a testament to human ingenuity. Yet, within this realm of boundless possibilities lies a paradox—a delicate equilibrium between the pursuit of innovation and the imperative of security. As technology permeates every facet of modern existence, the challenge lies in nurturing innovation while safeguarding against the vulnerabilities it may inadvertently create. This section explores the dynamic interplay between encouraging innovation and prioritizing security in cyberspace, delving into the symbiotic relationship between these dimensions, the challenges they present, strategies for fostering harmony, and the emergent role of technology as both catalyst and guardian.

The marriage of innovation and security is a nuanced dance—a choreography that harmonizes creativity with vigilance. Innovation, the driving force behind technological advancement, propels society forward by unraveling new horizons, birthing disruptive ideas, and transforming the very fabric of reality. Yet, in this fervent pursuit, the shadow of security casts its mantle. The vulnerabilities born from innovative breakthroughs expose digital landscapes to threats, from data breaches to cyberattacks. Navigating this duality—kindling the flames of innovation while erecting bastions of security—is a critical endeavor that transcends technological prowess and delves deep into the realms of ethics, governance, and human responsibility.

The digital frontier is a perpetual metamorphosis—an ever-shifting landscape where innovation transcends boundaries, industries, and disciplines. From artificial intelligence to blockchain, from cloud computing to the Internet of Things (IoT), the technological tapestry is replete with breakthroughs that redefine human potential. Innovators are the vanguard of this revolution, channeling their creativity to craft solutions that improve lives, streamline operations, and connect the world. Yet, as they shape tomorrow's reality, they encounter ethical and security considerations that necessitate a delicate balance between boundless innovation and the imperative of responsible creation.

Amidst the symphony of innovation, the clarion call of cybersecurity resounds—a call that beckons to shield digital landscapes from the unseen perils that innovation can unwittingly birth. Cybersecurity, the bastion against threats and breaches, is both sentinel and guide. Its role is twofold: to erect defenses that repel malevolent actors and instill a security culture that permeates every layer of digital creation. The partnership between innovation and cybersecurity is not adversarial; instead, it is a harmonious collaboration that ensures technology's potential is realized without compromising data integrity, privacy, or trust.

The dichotomy between innovation and security unfurls its complexities on a canvas painted with speed and progress. The rapid pace of innovation often outpaces the development of adequate security measures, rendering digital ecosystems susceptible to vulnerabilities. The emergence of zero-day vulnerabilities, the proliferation of malware, and the amplification of cyber threats in the wake of technological advancements underscore the challenge of synchronizing the tempo of innovation with the rhythm of security.

Fostering harmony between innovation and security requires a multifaceted approach encompassing education, collaboration, and integrating security at the heart of the creative process. Education empowers innovators with the knowledge to recognize security risks, prioritize responsible creation, and adhere to ethical considerations. Collaboration among stakeholders—innovators, cybersecurity experts, and policymakers—forges a collective endeavor to address challenges holistically. Embedding security as an integral part of the design and development phases ensures that the seeds of security are sown at the inception of innovation, yielding a crop of technologies fortified against cyber threats.

Ethical innovation emerges as a bridge that spans the chasm between innovation and security. By aligning innovative endeavors with ethical principles, innovators navigate the intricacies of security and shape technologies that amplify human well-being. Ethical considerations prompt innovators to contemplate their creations' potential consequences, evaluate their impact on society, and recognize the social contract that binds technological advancements to human betterment.

Regulatory frameworks and incentives are pivotal in encouraging the symbiosis of innovation and security. Regulations provide guardrails that guide innovation within ethical and security parameters, ensuring that innovations meet minimum safety and privacy standards. Incentives, from research grants to tax breaks, motivate innovators to prioritize security measures. Striking a balance between regulations that foster security and innovation-friendly policies that kindle creativity is the hallmark of a responsive governance framework.

The appearance of artificial intelligence (AI) and automation introduces a paradigm where technology itself becomes a guardian of security. AI-driven tools can analyze vast datasets, detect anomalies, and predict potential breaches, enhancing the proactive stance against cyber threats. Automation streamlines security operations, enabling swift responses to emerging threats. However, the ethical considerations of delegating security decisions to machines necessitate thoughtful design, transparency, and human oversight.

In the grand symphony of cyberspace, the notes of innovation and security are interwoven, each enhancing the other's melody. To encourage innovation while prioritizing security is to orchestrate a harmonious composition where the crescendo of creativity reverberates without compromising the safety of digital landscapes. It's a tapestry woven with ethical threads, a collaboration nurtured by education, a partnership fortified by collaboration, and a vision guided by the common goal of propelling society forward while safeguarding its digital horizons. The journey is one of shared responsibility—a journey where innovators wield their creativity as architects of a better future, and cybersecurity experts stand as guardians of integrity, ensuring that the symphony of innovation resounds without discord in the vast expanse of the digital realm.

CONCLUSION

Recap of key takeaways from the book

In the sprawling landscape of cyberspace, where innovation and security coalesce, the journey through our comprehensive book, "Cybersecurity Unveiled: The Art of Cyber Defense—A Comprehensive Guide to Protecting Your Data," has been one of exploration, discovery, and empowerment. From unraveling the intricacies of cyber threats to navigating the ethereal realm of encryption, from embracing responsible online behavior to fostering a culture of cybersecurity awareness, our odyssey has touched upon every facet of safeguarding the digital realm. As we conclude this journey, let us embark on a reflective journey—a recap of the key takeaways that have unfolded throughout this book, encapsulating the wisdom that empowers us to navigate the digital cosmos with vigilance, insight, and resilience.

The CIA Triad—Confidentiality, Integrity, and Availability—is the bedrock upon which cybersecurity strategies are built. Ensuring the confidentiality of sensitive data, preserving the integrity of information, and maintaining the availability of systems are the cornerstones of effective cybersecurity. This triad weaves a tapestry that safeguards the digital landscape against threats and vulnerabilities, guiding us to uphold the principles that define the essence of secure digital environments.

Encryption, an intricate realm of algorithms, emerges as the guardian of privacy in the digital age. Through the fusion of mathematics and technology, encryption renders sensitive data unintelligible to prying eyes, safeguarding it from interception and compromise. By understanding the principles of encryption and adopting it as a standard practice, we fortify our data against the omnipresent threats that loom in the digital horizon.

Access controls and authentication emerge as the sentinels at the gates of digital fortresses. By implementing stringent controls and multifaceted authentication mechanisms, we orchestrate a symphony of security restricting unauthorized entry, curbing the potential for breaches. Navigating the complexities of user access and verification is essential to ensuring that only those with rightful access traverse the digital thresholds.

The importance of data protection is etched in the annals of digital history. Safeguarding sensitive data from unauthorized access, misuse, or alteration is a perpetual quest that involves adhering to ethical practices, regulatory compliance, and robust security measures. Data protection is a testament to our commitment to preserving the trust of those who entrust us with their digital identities.

Cybersecurity is not static; it is an ever-evolving landscape where new threats emerge with each innovation. Embracing continuous learning becomes the anchor that tethers us to the tides of change. Staying updated on emerging threats, evolving defense strategies, and technological advancements equips us with the knowledge to navigate the digital currents with adaptability and resilience.

Ethical considerations illuminate the path of cybersecurity, shaping our choices, practices, and interactions within the digital realm. Prioritizing responsible online behavior, ethical research, and the well-being of individuals is a moral obligation that underscores the intersection of technology and humanity. Ethical guardianship serves as a compass that steers us away from practices that compromise the integrity of the digital landscape.

The delicate equilibrium between innovation and security underscores the transformative potential of technology. Encouraging innovation while prioritizing security is a collaborative endeavor—a partnership that harmonizes creativity with vigilance, disruption with stability. As technological breakthroughs reshape the world, the role of ethics, governance, and human responsibility emerges as a pivotal force in guiding the trajectory of progress.

The future of cybersecurity is an uncharted terrain—an expanse where AI-driven solutions, quantum computing, and evolving threat landscapes converge. Cybersecurity guardians must traverse these horizons with insight and ethical mindfulness as technology unfurls new possibilities. By fostering a culture of cybersecurity awareness, embracing ethical innovation, and adapting to the emerging tools of defense, we fortify our resilience against the uncertainties that lie ahead.

As we close the chapter on this comprehensive guide, let us remember that the journey through cyberspace is a collective responsibility. From individuals to organizations, educators to policymakers, and leaders to learners, we stand united in safeguarding the digital landscape. By embracing the key takeaways encapsulated within these virtual pages, we embrace the role of guardians, stewards, and advocates—nurturing a digital world where innovation and security intertwine to create a realm that reflects the best of human potential, aspirations, and integrity.

Encouragement for readers to implement cybersecurity practices

In the ever-evolving panorama of the digital world, where the boundaries of physical and virtual realities blur, the tapestry of our lives is woven with digital threads—communication, commerce, knowledge-sharing—all seamlessly interwoven within the fabric of cyberspace. Yet, beneath this façade of convenience and connectivity lies a landscape rife with threats, vulnerabilities, and unseen perils. In the chapters of this book, we have journeyed through the intricacies of cybersecurity, unraveling its nuances, strategies, and ethical dimensions. As we conclude, our mission transcends the realm of knowledge dissemination—it transforms into an earnest encouragement, a rallying cry, to embrace and implement cybersecurity practices that stand as the vanguard against digital threats. Let us delve into the essence of this encouragement—exploring why cybersecurity matters, the transformative power of individual action, strategies for integration, and the profound impact that united cybersecurity efforts can wield.

Cybersecurity isn't merely a technical discipline relegated to experts; it is the bedrock upon which digital trust is built. In a world where personal data is the currency of the digital realm, interconnected systems facilitate critical operations, and online interactions span the globe, cybersecurity is the guardian of integrity, privacy, and reliability. Consider the breaches that make headlines—the data leaks, the ransomware attacks, the phishing scams—each one punctuating cybersecurity's vital role in preserving the trust upon which our digital lives rest.

In the grand tapestry of cybersecurity, every individual is a thread that contributes to the resilience of the whole. The power of individual action cannot be understated. By implementing cybersecurity practices in our personal and professional lives, we amplify our collective defense against threats. A single compromised account can be a foothold for cybercriminals; a single unsecured device can become a breach conduit. However, when individuals choose to prioritize security—by adopting strong passwords, enabling two-factor authentication, recognizing phishing attempts, and practicing responsible online behavior—the collective impact is a formidable bulwark against threats.

Integrating cybersecurity into daily life is not daunting; it's a series of conscious choices that elevate our digital resilience. Begin by securing your devices with robust passwords that blend complexity and memorability.

Enable two-factor authentication to add layer of security to your online accounts. Stay vigilant against phishing attempts that masquerade as legitimate communications, and educate yourself about their telltale signs. Protect your personal data by limiting what you share online and being cautious about the platforms you entrust it to.

Regularly update your software as well as applications to ensure you have the most recent security patches. Embrace the culture of cybersecurity awareness, not as an obligation, but as a means of asserting your agency in the digital realm.

The allure of a safer digital world isn't realized in isolation—it's a collective aspiration that necessitates united efforts. Organizations, communities, educators, policymakers, and individuals alike form the symphony that resonates with the harmonies of cybersecurity. Organizations bolster their defenses to protect customer data and maintain trust. Communities share knowledge and resources, nurturing a culture of awareness.

Educators impart the fundamentals of cybersecurity to empower the digital citizens of tomorrow. Policymakers craft regulations and frameworks that set the standards for responsible practices. Individuals, like you, become the catalysts of change by choosing security over complacency.

The digital legacy we leave is an imprint of the choices we make today. Embracing cybersecurity practices is not just a response to current threats but a gesture shaping the future. It's a gesture that safeguards the data of future generations, preserves the integrity of digital interactions, and strengthens the foundation of trust upon which the digital world is built. It's a legacy that declares that we refused to be passive bystanders in the face of cyber threats. It's a legacy that reverberates with the message that our digital odyssey was characterized by innovation and ethical responsibility.

As we conclude this book, let us pause and reflect on the significance of our individual roles in the realm of cybersecurity. Your journey through these words has not been passive—it has been an initiation into a realm of agency, empowerment, and ethical mindfulness. By implementing cybersecurity practices, you become the architect of a safer digital world. You become the advocate for digital trust. You become the guardian of integrity. Whenever you choose security, you contribute to a digital narrative that reflects the best of human aspirations—an interconnected world where innovation is balanced by vigilance, convenience is shielded by responsibility, and progress is harmonized with ethical integrity. The journey continues beyond these pages, and your impact is immeasurable. So, as you navigate the complexity of cyberspace, do so with the conviction that your choices matter, your actions ripple, and your commitment to cybersecurity is the cornerstone of a digital future that is resilient, robust, and redolent with promise.

Final thoughts on the importance of cyber defense

In the ever-evolving landscape of the digital age, where lines between reality and virtuality blur, the importance of cyber defense stands as an immutable truth—a sentinel guarding against the unrelenting tide of cyber threats. Our journey through this book has explored cyber defense's intricacies, strategies, and ethical dimensions. As we stand at the crossroads of knowledge and action, let us delve into the culmination of our discourse—final thoughts on the resounding significance of cyber defense, its role in shaping the digital narrative, the imperative of global collaboration, and a reaffirmation of our shared responsibility in safeguarding the future.

Cyber defense isn't an isolated endeavor; it's the bedrock upon which the edifice of digital trust is erected. In a world where every click, keystroke, and transaction leaves a digital footprint, the importance of securing data, networks, and systems transcends mere technicality. It becomes a moral and ethical duty—a commitment to preserving the integrity of digital interactions, safeguarding sensitive information, and upholding the values that underpin the interconnected digital world. Just as the guardians of ancient citadels shielded their domains from external threats, cyber defense is the contemporary embodiment of that timeless duty—protecting the realm from unseen adversaries.

The digital narrative's trajectory is intertwined with cyber defense's efficacy. As technology becomes deeply ingrained in every facet of life, its transformative potential is both awe-inspiring and precarious. Innovations propel society forward, enabling us to communicate, collaborate, and create in ways previously unimagined. However, these innovations are a double-edged sword; they invite progress and vulnerability. The narrative unfolds is shaped by how effectively we can wield technology while mitigating the risks it introduces. Cyber defense provides the canvas on which this narrative is painted, coloring it with shades of resilience, integrity, and security.

Cyber threats transcend borders, languages, and ideologies—a stark reminder of the interconnectedness of the digital realm. In this interconnectedness lies the imperative of global collaboration. Cyber defense isn't a localized endeavor; it's a global responsibility that necessitates cooperation among nations, industries, and individuals. Cyberattacks that target critical infrastructure, compromise personal data, or disrupt digital services underscore the necessity of collective defense. By sharing threat intelligence, collaborating on cybersecurity policies, and fostering a culture of responsible digital citizenship, the global community can forge an unbreakable shield against cyber threats.

Ethics stand as a guiding star in the realm of cyber defense, illuminating the path of responsible action. The choices we make in the domain of cybersecurity are not merely technical decisions; they are reflections of our values, commitments, and obligations. Ethical considerations prompt us to balance the imperatives of security with the preservation of individual privacy, to prioritize responsible innovation over reckless disruption, and to cultivate a culture of cybersecurity awareness that safeguards the well-being of all stakeholders. The ethical horizon of cyber defense navigates us away from the abyss of shortsighted actions and steers us toward the shores of collective betterment.

Cyber defense is a shared responsibility that transcends roles, titles, and expertise. From the individual who secures their online accounts with strong passwords to the cybersecurity expert who devises robust defense strategies, from the organization that invests in cutting-edge technologies to the policymaker who crafts regulations to protect citizens, every stakeholder plays a role in this digital defense orchestra. A chain is only as strong as its weakest link, in the same way the digital landscape is fortified only when every participant shoulders their responsibility. It's a responsibility to educate, advocate, and act—to shape a world where the advancement of security mirrors the advancement of technology.

As we bring this book to a close, let us reflect on the profound impact of cyber defense on the digital horizon. The journey through these words has not merely been an intellectual pursuit; it has been an invitation to join the ranks of guardians—guardians of integrity, guardians of resilience, and guardians of the future. The importance of cyber defense is etched not only in the lines of code that define our digital infrastructure but also in the values that define our humanity. It is a testament to our commitment to the well-being of digital citizens, the preservation of digital interactions, and the elevation of digital society to unimagined heights. So, as you traverse the virtual expanse, remember that every action you take to bolster cyber defense echoes through the corridors of the digital world, resonating with the promise of a safer, more secure, and more ethically fortified digital realm. The journey continues beyond these words, and your role as a guardian stands resolute—steering the course of cyberspace toward a future where innovation and security dance in harmonious cadence.

Thank you for buying and reading/listening to our book. If you found this book useful/helpful please take a few minutes and leave a review on the platform where you purchased our book. Your feedback matters greatly to us.